T0318918

Cambridge Elements ☰

Elements in Health Communication
edited by
Louise Cummings
The Hong Kong Polytechnic University

WORSE THAN IGNORANCE

The Challenge of Health Misinformation

Peter J. Schulz
University of Lugano and Nanyang Technological University

Kent Nakamoto
University of Lugano

Shaftesbury Road, Cambridge CB2 8EA, United Kingdom

One Liberty Plaza, 20th Floor, New York, NY 10006, USA

477 Williamstown Road, Port Melbourne, VIC 3207, Australia

314–321, 3rd Floor, Plot 3, Splendor Forum, Jasola District Centre,
New Delhi – 110025, India

103 Penang Road, #05–06/07, Visioncrest Commercial, Singapore 238467

Cambridge University Press is part of Cambridge University Press & Assessment,
a department of the University of Cambridge.

We share the University's mission to contribute to society through the pursuit of
education, learning and research at the highest international levels of excellence.

www.cambridge.org
Information on this title: www.cambridge.org/9781009467902

DOI: 10.1017/9781009289542

© Peter J. Schulz and Kent Nakamoto 2024

First published 2024

A catalogue record for this publication is available from the British Library.

ISBN 978-1-009-46790-2 Hardback
ISBN 978-1-009-28952-8 Paperback
ISSN 2754-1045 (online)
ISSN 2754-1037 (print)

Cambridge University Press & Assessment has no responsibility for the persistence
or accuracy of URLs for external or third-party internet websites referred to in this
publication and does not guarantee that any content on such websites is, or will
remain, accurate or appropriate.

Worse Than Ignorance

The Challenge of Health Misinformation

Elements in Health Communication

DOI: 10.1017/9781009289542
First published online: April 2024

Peter J. Schulz
University of Lugano and Nanyang Technological University

Kent Nakamoto
University of Lugano

Author for correspondence: Peter J. Schulz, peter.schulz@usi.ch

Abstract: This Element considers health misinformation and the problems it presents. The evolving communication context—changing doctor-patient relationships and developments in information technology—presents patients with a vastly enriched information landscape and new challenges to patients navigating it. These challenges are magnified as growing patient empowerment and autonomy have increased expectations for patient involvement in medical decisions. In this context, the ways people approach presented information, learn from it, understand it, and use it, exacerbate the risk that they become misinformed—believing things that are inimical to improved health. Moreover, these same processes make it difficult to correct such beliefs. Approaches building on trust between patient and professional exemplify improved communication to increase accurate patient knowledge and understanding in the service of better health. This title is also available as Open Access on Cambridge Core.

Keywords: misinformation in health, internet health information, health literacy, communication failure, shared decision-making

ISBNs: 9781009467902 (HB), 9781009289528 (PB), 9781009289542 (OC)
ISSNs: 2754-1045 (online), 2754-1037 (print)

Contents

Preface

This Element reads as a catalogue of disappointment. The twenty-first century dawned with dreams of information technology enabling better health through new services and support for doctors and patients alike. 'Glitches' and false starts were explained away as minor irrelevances or beginners' difficulties. Yet even as online information and commerce have exploded, the promise of improved health communication remains a mirage – beautiful but illusory.

Health communication failures persist, and they can no longer be explained by the novelty of the tremendous communication apparatus that surrounds us. This Element explores the failings and the risks those failures pose for patients and healthcare professionals. Origins of these difficulties are traced to the nature of knowledge and the problem of linking it to 'reality', and some of the psychological processes that lead people to accept misinformation are considered. Focused attempts to address the problem – education, campaigns, programs – are discussed, and structural concepts such as health literacy and patient empowerment are scrutinized both for the help they might provide and for their role in the perpetuation of the difficulties. In addition, the special capability, responsibility, and interest of doctors to move against communication failures are considered as a key resource to combat health misinformation.

What emerges is not a single culprit who stands in the way of applying sound knowledge to achieve better health, but a network of influences and conditions damaging (purposely or not) people's ability to distinguish accurate from inaccurate information. The problem brings us back to a perennial question – what are good reasons for knowing one is right, overlain with the modern objective of actually improving health. The problem of misinformation, then, isn't a 'glitch' but a foundational problem for new technology and health information. While we cannot offer a broad solution, we note central preconditions for and promising examples of improved communication and understanding.

Introduction: The Problem of Knowledge Failures in Health

Since the discovery of microorganisms as causal agents in infections, medicine has been transformed by immense technological achievements – from vaccination to prevent disease, antibiotics to treat disease, and imaging methods, starting with X-rays, to diagnose disease. Today's three-dimensional imaging that visualizes physiological function as well as anatomical structure has revolutionized medical diagnosis. New laparoscopic surgical techniques return patients to normal life in days rather than months, and a vast armamentarium of new medicines has revolutionized even the treatment of fearsome diseases like cancer as well as many conditions perhaps less frightening but still debilitating.

Alongside the impacts of medical innovation, there have been extraordinary achievements in improving public health. Through coordinated efforts, smallpox was eradicated in 1977, and polio remains endemic in only a few countries in the world. Clean water and improved sanitation have virtually eradicated diseases like cholera and dysentery in large parts of the world. These public health successes involved much more than medical innovation. They required extensive programs of education and persuasion, leading to community and individual acceptance and participation. The success of eradication programs, for example, depends on rapid reporting of new cases, acceptance of vaccination, and adoption of allied practices like quarantining.

In tandem with these developments, the very concept of health has evolved, entailing far more than the biomedical treatment of disease. Health today is recognized as a profoundly personal concept that entails physical, mental, and social well-being.[1] The importance of this enriched concept of health lies in the fact that we live in an information-rich age that makes people ever more capable of autonomous action with the potential to improve their health. To realize this potential, people not only have to be made aware of their biomedical needs but they also must be persuaded that those needs are important to their health goals and be motivated to adopt the appropriate actions. By all accounts, the difficulties faced by health professionals and institutions in accomplishing these tasks have limited the realization of the potential of medical technology and public health expertise.[2]

A recent vivid example is the development of vaccines for Covid-19 – a technological tour de force accomplished in an extraordinarily short time, building on decades of research on related organisms and new RNA-based approaches to vaccination. Yet, despite its enormous benefits, vaccination adoption has been far from universal. Even in April 2022, fifteen months after the introduction of Covid vaccines, barely half of the eligible population in the European Union had received a primary vaccine course plus one booster, and 25% remained completely unvaccinated.[3] Such problems are by no means novel. As of 2003, only 50% of patients in developed countries with chronic health conditions adhered to treatment protocols, and even fewer did so in developing countries.[4] In short, people are making health choices too often to their own detriment.

The causes of problematic health choices are, in part, systemic. Access to primary healthcare is cited as a major factor. Global economic inequality limits the availability of healthcare services. This is compounded by a lack of education that impairs people's ability to read and understand health information.

However, even in wealthy countries with high rates of literacy and extensive healthcare systems, innovations and new tools fail to provide anticipated benefits due to human factors. Technological innovations achieve little if people refuse to accept them, particularly if they deny the health problem is serious or that the innovation is safe and efficacious. In recent cases, these beliefs are coupled with suspicion of government and institutions like business (Big Pharma), distrust of 'experts', and feelings of powerlessness and insecurity. As a result, too many people reject technological innovations – they find their own information, make their own choices, and pursue their own treatments.[5]

The issue we examine in this Element arises from these decisions. What problems can emerge when people seek health information? Prior to the dominance of the internet, traditional family lore and experience provided health guidance until the patient grew too sick. Then, people sought the advice of health professionals. Very few would seek information from medical journals, so the professional served as an information gatekeeper and, to a large extent, guaranteed the accuracy and relevance of presented information. Of course, some information might be omitted, and the information presented could lean towards a particular interpretation or favour a particular recommendation. Nevertheless, the professional's goal was to tailor the information to that patient's health problems and their capacity to comprehend, accept, and respond to them.

When patients use the internet to find health information, at least two problems arise. First, the information is not tailored to the patient. This means that the patient must assess the information's relevance and applicability to their specific health condition. However, the patient's health expertise is limited. The patient is well attuned to his specific symptoms and circumstances. But, few patients have the medical background knowledge to assess for themselves the relevance and meaning of information for their case. Second, the internet provides little guarantee of the quality of information presented. Conflicting information appears without filters or other forms of validation. Systems are proposed for rating the reliability of websites (e.g., HON rating), but they lack clear criteria, and such criteria may not exist relative to personalized needs. Again, patients are left to make their own judgements regarding information veracity. The physician's expert knowledge and ability to make educated judgements about what information is critical to the diagnosis and treatment of that patient is missing. Those patients who choose to 'go it alone' often overlook these differences. Moreover, the patient is often unaware of what he or she doesn't know – including potentially critical information. Thus, patients may acquire and rely on information that is incorrect or inapplicable or may remain ignorant of important information. These problems – ignorance and misinformation – are the central phenomena we consider here.

Misinformation in the field of health can spread with or without intention. In the latter case, we may speak of error. The intentional provision of misinformation is also called disinformation. The global foray of Covid-19 disinformation has drawn much attention to the influence of falsehoods promulgated worldwide. Prominent news reports highlight the resulting problems. As Covid-19 cases increased rapidly in Iran, disinformation was circulated claiming that gargling or drinking alcohol prevented or cured the infection. As a result, 728 deaths from methanol poisoning were recorded in Iran between March and April 2020 compared to 66 during the same period the year before.[6]

For the consumer, being misinformed is one type of knowledge failure – holding and believing false information,[7] with all its attendant problems.[8–10] A second well-explored failure is ignorance – the lack of knowledge. We therefore distinguish three groups: (1) individuals who think they have sound knowledge of a matter and get it right, (2) individuals who think they have sound knowledge as well but get it wrong, and (3) individuals who lack knowledge and know it. The irony is that the people in groups 1 and 2 – actual opposites – often feel similar about their knowledge.[11]

It is also important to distinguish misinformation from being uninformed – also potentially costly and the focus of much research on health literacy. People with a lower ability to read and understand medical information display less knowledge and comprehension of healthcare resources, lower rates of compliance with medical advice, and worse outcomes including increased hospitalization and health costs.[12] The goal of improving health grounds health literacy – understanding may be subjective, but not to the point that established facts are ignored or distorted or new 'facts' invented. Health literacy implies understanding of what is important to a health decision so that the appropriate skills can be summoned. 'Self-examination and the application of skills might lead one to decide not to follow specific treatment advice or to negotiate for changing it in a way that better suits one's life. However, if literacy is to lead to better health outcomes and physical well-being, the literate person cannot distort or ignore relevant facts.' (p. 310).[13]

From antiquity through the nineteenth century, patients' medical knowledge and their ability to gain more of it were not clinical concerns. Knowledge was what the physician brought to the consultation, and ironically much of it was erroneous. More recent efforts to empower patients and involve them in medical decision-making have created their own problems, and Section 1 considers the societal and technological changes that fostered them. Patient empowerment enables patients – indeed expects them – to participate more actively in healthcare decisions, seeking to improve patient–clinician relationships, patient satisfaction, and health outcomes.[14] Active patient participation is also an unavoidable (perhaps even subconscious) product of the availability of vast quantities of medical information on the internet and social media, in direct-to-consumer advertising of prescription pharmaceuticals, and in direct-to-consumer marketing of medical tests and screens.

Patient empowerment also highlights the importance of health literacy as a crucial requirement to enable people to make choices that advance their health goals.[15] Unfortunately, as vividly reflected in the controversies over Covid-19 vaccination and treatment, seeking to improve literacy by providing accurate and adequate information cannot ensure that patients make healthy choices. The nature and genesis of knowledge failures and the limits of literacy and empowerment to counteract them form the central issues of the next three sections. Section 2 presents more systematic considerations of knowledge, its links to external evidence, and potential failures. Section 3 considers communication processes and their role in exacerbating knowledge failures, specifically the problem of misinformation. Section 4 considers the challenges facing those seeking to prevent or repair misinformation and the reasons for failure of health literacy and other educational programs as well as public health campaigns to achieve these goals.

In the face of these challenges, countering mistaken beliefs must be more than addressing gaps in patient knowledge. Even well-designed communication campaigns fail. This suggests a central role for the health professional – especially the physician, as we discuss in Section 5. There, we consider the nature and role of trust, arguing that a trusting, collaborative doctor–patient relationship can play a critical role in promoting accurate patient knowledge, understanding, and healthy choices.

Health misinformation is a natural, if regrettable, product of human information processing, exacerbated by modern communication technology. It will continue to challenge our health and the healthcare professionals who work with us to improve it. Correcting misinformation is often difficult, and there is no panacea, only strategies to leverage the same tools that lead to being misinformed to counter it, in the hope that over the longer term, people will better understand how to improve their health.

1 The Growth of Health Misinformation

Medical misinformation has always been with us. Aside from quackery, it can be seen in theories later disproven and practices based on folk tradition. Hippocrates in ancient Greece held that health was governed by four humours – blood, phlegm, yellow bile, and black bile. The four were balanced in a healthy person; an increase or decrease of a humour was linked to illness.[16] This view, refined by Galen, dominated medical thought through the Medieval period. Fever was thought to be due to an excess of blood, so to regain balance the excess had to be discharged, which was achieved by bleeding the patient. Bloodletting as a medical treatment continued to be applied in Western medicine through much of the nineteenth century.[17] Unproven treatments found in traditional, folk, and domestic medicine also rely on questionable theories. Many people identified two types of problems – those requiring getting rid of poison and those requiring restoring energy.[18] Thus, homemade teas using various plant materials were taken either as purgatives (e.g., sassafras as a diuretic, buckthorn syrup as a laxative) or as a tonic (e.g., bitter herbs for the treatment of 'rheumatism').[19] More recently, the internet and social media have facilitated the rapid spread of misinformation. For example, Cannabidiol (CBD) has been shown in clinical studies to have value in treating two rare forms of epilepsy in children. However, the myriad of uses for CBD on the internet, including treatment of pain, anxiety, depression, and inflammation, lack clinical evidence and rely heavily on anecdotal reports.[20,21]

The focus of this section is the increased availability of information – accurate and inaccurate – to the patient or consumer. The issue of appropriately informing patients about their health problems and treatments is venerable. Discussion of the appropriate roles of physician and patient and the information to be provided in the context of medical treatment date back to Hippocrates, and until recently, physicians held a position of authority that allowed them to act as information gatekeepers deciding what patients needed to know. However, the landscape of patient knowledge has changed profoundly over the past fifty years and with it the dimensions of the problem of misinformation. First, the idea of patient autonomy has undergone a radical expansion, starting with changing expectations about informing patients. Second, the internet has made vast amounts of information relating to health immediately available to everyone and has resulted in the widespread adoption of the internet as a major, often primary, source of health and medical information. These changes have exacerbated the problem of health misinformation.

The Evolving Doctor–Patient Relationship

The relationship between a healthcare professional – most notably a physician – and a patient involves a necessary asymmetry in knowledge. Knowledge and skill gained through extensive training and experience define healthcare professionals and are the reasons they are consulted. The knowledge held by the professional but not by the patient is the basis on which the professional can assist the patient. However, it has far-reaching effects; physicians 'not only advise actions but also evaluate the nature of reality and experience, including the 'needs' of those who consult them'. Their expertise allows them 'to interpret signs and symptoms, to diagnose health or illness, to name diseases, and to offer prognoses . . .. By shaping the patients' understanding of their own experience, physicians create the conditions under which their advice seems appropriate' (pp. 13–14).[22] Beyond assistance, then, this superior knowledge forms a basis for the professional's authority – a recognition by patients that they need to defer to professional judgements and comply with the physician's recommendations because of predicted negative outcomes for noncompliance.

Underlying this doctor–patient relationship is the patient's trust that the physician has the expertise and the motivation to help them. That physician's expertise can, in fact, help the patient is due to the advances in medical science and technology.[18] Beginning in the late nineteenth century, these advances propelled scientific medicine. In 1882, building on advances in microscopic pathology, Koch identified the Tuberculosis bacillus and the germ theory of disease. Antisepsis, along with anaesthesia, advanced the possibilities of surgical intervention. The X-ray entered medical practice in the early twentieth century, greatly increasing the physician's ability to diagnose illness. Pain management was an early advance with the introduction of morphine in 1844 and aspirin in 1899 as well as barbiturates to calm patients and treat epileptic seizures in 1903. As for actually curing patients of organic disease, diphtheria antitoxin was introduced in the early 1890s. However, it was the discovery of antibiotics – sulfa drugs in the late 1930s, penicillin in 1941, and later in the 1940s streptomycin, chloramphenicol, and tetracycline – that allowed physicians to change the course of disease. The physician's expertise thus made a bigger difference; it also increased the knowledge asymmetry. Patients had to take more on trust, but this was rarely a problem as trust in physicians also increased.

The knowledge asymmetry limits the patient's ability to gauge a provider's expertise, so society (through peer professional groups and state regulation) seeks to ensure a sufficient level of expertise by mandating certain requirements. Physicians must demonstrate through formal education, supervised experience, and examination a sufficient level of competence before being licensed by the state to practice medicine. Practising without a license is criminal. While these credentials and sanctions seek to ensure professional competence, society also seeks to prevent abuse of the knowledge asymmetry by making credentialed professionals legally liable for malpractice – acting against the interests of the person seeking their assistance. These credentials and consequences lend an institutional legitimacy that adds to the physician's authority in the health domain.

Physician abuse of that authority constitutes malpractice, and legal cases in the US date back to the early 1800s. However, while numerous notorious malpractice cases can be cited, the legal structure is a clumsy approach to addressing the broader societal concerns regarding professional relationships. Even without legal malpractice, patients can feel dissatisfied with their medical care or with their interactions with health professionals. These broader considerations are discussed in terms of (bio)medical ethics that form part of the physician's training, and which are maintained as principles by professional societies. In modern terms, Beauchamp and Childress present four moral principles guiding professional action: '(1) *respect for autonomy* (a norm of respecting and supporting autonomous decisions), (2) *nonmaleficence* (a norm of avoiding the causation of harm), (3) *beneficence* (a group of norms pertaining to relieving, lessening, or preventing harm and providing benefits and balancing benefits against risks and costs), and (4) *justice* (a group of norms for fairly distributing benefits, risks, and costs)' (p. 13).[23] Respect for autonomy and justice grew in importance only recently, while nonmaleficence and beneficence have long been important considerations.[24] They are enshrined, for example, in the Hippocratic Oath: 'I will use treatment to help the sick according to my ability and judgment, but never with a view to injury and wrong-doing.'[25]

Importantly, these norms apply to the physician. The physician is to confer benefits and avoid doing harm, but the requirements of the patients are either absent or implicit. In fact, because of the knowledge asymmetry and its consequences, the patient was long viewed as dependent – either as a passive recipient of treatments or as one who needed to be managed to comply with and adhere to the physician's recommendations. In this arrangement, appropriate information for the patient was determined by the physician and a common practice and even recommended norm was to withhold information that would cast doubt on the physician's preferred treatment option.[26] To admit or imply uncertainty could confuse patients or lead them to question the physician's treatment recommendation and become less compliant.[27] This type of relationship has been described as paternalistic and, by the 1980s, came to be viewed by many as incomplete, if not inappropriate. This was not only an ethical concern. Shorter argues that the advances in the doctor's ability to treat patients led, paradoxically, to a decrease in their trust in doctors. Patients consult physicians more often for more symptoms, which increases the pressure on physicians to see more patients, so the time available to explore the patient's concerns shrinks. By the 1980s, the average consultation with a family doctor lasted 11 minutes,[18] and a recent international review found that average primary care physician consultations ranged from under 1 minute to 22 minutes.[28] In response, physicians focused on the organic problems at the expense of the patient as a thinking, feeling person – one reason patient trust in physicians declined.

In this context, principles of patient autonomy and justice entered the calculus of the doctor–patient relationship. It is important to remember that healthcare professionals – physicians, nurses, pharmacists – were still primary sources of medical and health information. The internet lay in the future, and accessing medical journals required visiting an academic library, and few lay readers would understand the technical information found there. Media coverage of health was selective. General circulation magazines focused on health were novel. In the US, for example, a general circulation magazine *Hygeia*, later *Today's Health*, was published by the American Medical Association from 1923 to 1976. *Prevention,* billed as 'a medical journal for the people', launched in 1950, but other popular magazines of this genre came much later. *Health* (an American magazine focused on women's health) was launched in 1981; *Men's Health* followed six years later, in 1987. As such, healthcare professionals continued to act as information gatekeepers.

Nevertheless, *patient empowerment* gained a prominent place in visions of optimal health following the emergence of the Ottawa Charter from a 1986 international conference, which proposed that 'health promotion is the process of enabling people to increase control over, and to improve, their health'.[29] For some, this vision took a relational (e.g., doctor–patient) dimension – emphasizing the need for more egalitarian structures and a more equitable distribution of power between practitioners and patients.[30] Others took a more individualistic view, focusing on informed choice,[14] or on patient experience of feelings of power, control, or greater self-esteem.[31]

Patient Empowerment, Literacy, and Autonomy

Whether structural or individual, patient empowerment implies the active participation of patients in making decisions about their health and healthcare. The appeal of patient empowerment rests on three different traditions of thinking. It is advanced first on ethical grounds, complementing the physician's norm of respect for patient autonomy – to increase patients' personal autonomy in decision-making related to their health. A second reason for the growing interest in patient empowerment has been the view that citizens should participate in and take responsibility for their healthcare to control healthcare costs.[32] Third, and perhaps most importantly, patient empowerment is advocated as improving health outcomes.[33] These arguments ground a normative vision of 'patient-centred' collaborative decision-making involving healthcare professionals and patients.

Despite these arguments, debate arose regarding the operational meaning and desirability of various aspects of patient empowerment. Salmon and Hall, for example, discuss findings regarding patient-controlled analgesia – a seemingly clear case of empowerment. However, patients noted that, rather than control, the benefit was less need to bother the nurses, that is, it 'disempowered patients by inhibiting assertion of their own needs from clinical staff'.[34] Thus, it is important to understand the patient's perspective. In a population study in the US, 96% of respondents wished to be offered choices and to be asked for their opinions, although over half preferred to leave the decision to their physician.[35] A patient's desire for information may derive from concerns other than decision-making, for example, wanting to know the reasons for a recommendation along with an assurance that the range of possible options has been considered.[36] From the standpoint of the physician, as Vinson notes:

> This leads to a classic tension in patient care: physicians believe they have remedies that will ameliorate the patient's condition. The physician must square these interventions with the desires of the patient, which have been increasingly marked by consumerism and the assertion of their own expertise based on lived experience and independent research[37] (p. 1368)

As such, doctor–patient interactions are heavily influenced by the knowledge asymmetry,[38] but must negotiate rather than dictate a treatment plan. Vinson describes the result as 'constrained collaboration'. We return to this point in discussing bounding patient empowerment and literacy.

If empowering patients is to lead to good decisions and improved health outcomes, patients must be adequately informed. This need for better-informed patients led to an allied focus on health literacy. *Health literacy* first appeared in a 1974 paper calling for minimal health education standards for all grade levels in the US.[39] Since then, a stream of descriptive research has sought to examine the concept of health literacy, its measurement, and the problem of low health literacy. Health literacy (specifically functional literacy – the ability to read and comprehend health information) has received a great deal of attention because of its proposed impact on individual health and healthcare costs. There is little disagreement that health literacy is crucial in managing one's health. Studies of low health literacy associate it with lack of knowledge, decreased comprehension, lack of understanding and use of preventive services, poorer self-reported health, lower compliance rates, increased hospitalizations, and increased health costs.[12,40] Unsurprisingly, patients with low literacy experience poorer outcomes – health status, intermediate disease markers, measures of morbidity, general health status, and use of health resources.[41–44]

A growing body of research has focused on developing interventions to improve health literacy or limit the problems posed for people with low health literacy, with most of the literature advocating education as a key to health promotion and disease prevention. For example, diabetes education programs improved patient knowledge of diabetes and recommended dietary principles as well as key metabolic parameters (glycosylated haemoglobin, blood sugar, and urine sugar).[45] Programs included videotaped information, organized learning activities, community-based educational and self-help programs, and intensive education. Beyond education, convenient home-use glucose meters also became available.

Improving health literacy presents a complex problem of providing not only sufficient information, but also providing it in a way that is comprehensible and usable by the patient. This complexity can be seen, for example, in concerns for what constitutes informed consent in medical settings and how it is to be achieved.[46,47]

Informing Patients

Informed patient consent to medical treatment has been fundamental to discussions of patient autonomy. The idea of consent to treatment was formally recognized as early as 1914 in a US Supreme Court judgment that held performing surgery without the patient's consent to be assault, rendering the surgeon liable for damages.[24] However, this did not address the question of what had to be disclosed to the patient to inform their consent decision. *Informed consent* did not appear until 1957 in a California appellate decision,[26] and has been debated from both legal and ethical standpoints ever since. Over that period, informed consent has shifted from a basis of beneficence to one of autonomy. Under beneficence, the physician sought to provide medical benefits, and information was provided to support that provision. Today, the physician is expected to provide a great deal more information to support patient decision-making out of respect for the patient's autonomy. Withholding information and lying to the patient are, of course, inconsistent with this view.

At first glance, this vision would argue for complete transparency – the physician should tell the patient everything. Consistent with this view, patients have increasing access to their medical records. Particularly with the increased use of electronic medical records, patient access has been mandated by law in many countries. In the UK, the NHS App allows a patient to view much of their GP medical record, including laboratory and radiology reports, clinical notes, and doctor–patient communications. Similarly, in the US, patients have a right to access medical records, case notes, billing and payment records, including insurance, laboratory tests, and radiology reports and images.

This stance raises three questions: What does 'everything' include? Is it possible to tell the patient everything? Is telling the patient everything the best way to support patient autonomy? Because the patient has far less medical expertise as a background to use the physician's disclosures, 'everything' includes much more than a diagnosis, prognosis, and possible treatments and their benefits and risks. To make sense of this information, relevant background information must be provided as well. If the decision outcome is to serve the patient's concerns and goals, information may have to be interpreted relative to them. The information would also have to be tailored to the patient's level of health literacy. However, both tailoring and interpretation could be construed as manipulation by the physician, so the problem remains of how to present this information best.

Even if complete transparency on the part of the physician were possible, could the patient use the information to make an informed decision? Some research suggests that providing too much information can be overwhelming, leading to greater reliance on heuristics or rules of thumb that simplify the choice but can result in worse outcomes.[48] Thus, autonomy viewed as independent patient decision-making presents dangers. At the other extreme, Tauber suggests that asking the physician to make the treatment decision (as in 'if you were me, what would you do?') does not automatically imply loss of autonomy. The patient is making an autonomous judgement that the physician can be trusted to use knowledge and expertise to seek the best outcome for the patient. If appropriately informing the patient is this complicated in the structured and well-meaning environment of informed consent, how much more complex is the issue of informing patients in the outside world?

The Changing Information Environment

The evolution of thinking about patient autonomy, empowerment, and literacy began in a relatively controlled information environment. Patients were dependent on healthcare professionals for information, and professional, legal, and ethical considerations ensured that the patient's well-being was paramount. However, beginning in the 1980s the health information environment changed – first with the rise of direct-to-consumer advertising (DTCA) of prescription drugs and then with the advent of health information on the internet. These developments have increased the informational challenges facing patients.

Direct-to-Consumer Advertising of Prescription Medications

Direct-to-consumer advertising – the promotion of prescription medicines to the public in the lay media, is allowed only in the US and New Zealand. There have been industry efforts in many countries to relax restrictions on DTCA,[49,50] notably in the European Union although DTCA there remains forbidden. In the US, it was not until 1981 that Merck ran the first print advertisement for its pneumococcus vaccine.[51] The first broadcast ad ran in 1983. Following a clarification of Food and Drug Administration regulations in 1985 and relaxation of the information requirements in 1999 and 2004, both print and broadcast DTCA grew rapidly. US DTCA expenditures increased over fivefold from around $800 million in 1996 to $4.8 billion in 2008.[52]

One might ask why firms would advertise products that only physicians can prescribe for patients, but DTCA in the US is effective in increasing sales and represents one of the fastest-growing forms of pharmaceutical marketing.[53] The US General Accounting Office estimates that 8.5 million consumers annually request and receive a prescription for a particular drug from their physician in response to seeing DTCA.[54] It is cited by many patients as prompting questions for their doctor, including asking about a specific brand.[55]

The core of the debate over allowing DTCA is whether the advertising benefits patients and should be promoted, or places patients at risk and should be curtailed or abolished (and not introduced in other countries).[56,57] DTCA is regulated, and in the US, the ad must not be misleading, must provide information that relates to the medications' uses, and include balanced information about the medication's benefits and particularly about its risks. According to promoters of DTCA, pharmaceutical companies have more accurate, balanced, and scientifically based information than any other sources.[58] As such, they are in an exclusive position to provide people with adequate information on the safe use of medication, as well as to create effective knowledge for evaluating the benefits and risks of drug products, and generally assisting people in managing their health autonomously and appropriately.[59] Also, DTCA has been credited with decreasing the under-diagnosis and under-treatment of medical conditions.[57,60]

Opponents emphasize that DTCA may misinform and mislead patients,[61] partly because it overemphasizes the drug benefits and partly because risk information is not properly presented.[62,63] In this view, DTCA's primary aim is to create name and brand recognition with the goal of increasing the use of the advertised products. Pharmaceutical companies are further criticized for promoting medicalization in DTCA[64] and disease mongering.[65] DTCA is depicted as being devoid of value in increasing patient literacy but rather as encouraging drug-overutilization to increase the financial gains of pharmaceutical firms.

From the standpoint of providing health information, DTCA differs from professional advice. The information provided by DTCA is no longer customized to each recipient. While a doctor uses the diagnosis of the individual patient to guide his or her advice, advertising messages are uniform. The uses, benefits, and risks of the medication are presented, and the consumer is left to decide whether to seek it. Further, because one primary goal of advertising is to increase demand for the advertised drug, the presentation of information is naturally favourable. Information regarding risks and contraindications is typically presented in small type and technical language (print) or in very rapid speech with no visual support (broadcast). As suggested by opponents of DTCA, this places consumers at some risk of misunderstanding the advertising message (e.g., the appropriateness of the medication for them) and for suffering patients' potential motivation to focus on benefits rather than risks. As in the case of informed consent, increasing the amount of information provided does not automatically benefit consumers and patients. Thus, even good intentions (the health professional) and regulation (DTCA) cannot ensure that the content and presentation of information will best serve the patient or consumer. This issue is magnified in the absence of such constraints, leading us to the fundamental changes to the health information environment brought by the internet.

The Internet and the Changing Landscape of Health Information

For those who have grown up with the internet, life before it is a quaint anachronism characterized by the inefficiencies of standardized information – paper telephone directories issued annually and out of date by the time they appeared, paper maps for planning trips with no customized guidance, and news limited to a few broadcasters, newspapers, and magazines. Much information was simply not available – health information included. Getting information about health problems meant making an appointment with the doctor and meeting face-to-face. Email existed in various proprietary forms from the 1980s but even in 1997, the most popular email services were Microsoft's Hotmail, with a mere 11 million users, and AOL, with 10 million.[66]

The technology underlying the internet evolved from developments dating back to the 1960s but only came into being as we know it today in the early 1990s. The basic tools that enabled the World Wide Web, developed by Tim Berners-Lee, were released in 1991.[67] Use of and users of the internet grew phenomenally rapidly. In 1995, there were an estimated 16 million internet users.[68] Web browsers and search engines had been introduced. Commerce entered the internet in 1994 with the first banner ad by AT&T and in 1995, Amazon.com was launched as one of the earliest exclusively online retailers. Blogs were launched, as were online communities, precursors of social media. By 2000, there were an estimated 361 million internet users; by 2010, that had grown to 2 billion; by 2021, over 5 billion or some 66% of the world's population.[69] Social media is a relative latecomer. MySpace, in 2004, was the first social media site to reach a million users. Facebook launched in 2004 and grew by 2019 to 2.3 billion users.[70] The digital world we take for granted today is barely thirty years old.

Health organizations were early adopters of the internet as a medium for delivering information. Medscape, a site providing peer-reviewed information for medical professionals, was launched in 1995. WebMD, the most popular health information site in the US, was founded in 1996. In addition to informational sources, the internet has also seen the development of many web-based educational sites focused on the needs of specific patient groups. For example, an online Arthritis Self-Management Program developed by Lorig and colleagues at Stanford University is built around a six-week series of online sessions focused on tools participants could use to manage pain and improve function.[71]

These developments have been accompanied by profound changes in consumer behaviour that have made the internet a powerful force in the provision of health information. By 2007, over 70% of US adults used the internet and between 75% and 80% of them had searched for health information online at least once.[72] Online information often led patients to ask doctors new questions or to get a second opinion. Among patients with chronic conditions, 75% indicated that the information affects a decision about treating illness. In short, in a little more than a decade, the internet became a major force in informing patients about health and medical concerns. By 2012, 81% of US adults reported using the internet and 72% of them had looked for health information online in the past year.[73] An Australian survey of 2,944 patients found that 63.4% accessed the internet in the previous month and 28.1% sought health information.[74] Older patients were less likely to use the internet, as were those who were socioeconomically disadvantaged. By 2019, according to the National Cancer Institute Health Information National Trends Survey (HINTS), an estimated 72.7% of people who looked for information about health or medicine went to the internet first; 38.7% had watched a health-related YouTube video in the last year; 9.5% had participated in an online support group for people with a particular health issue. By 2020, 84.6% had used a health or wellness app.

The popularity of the internet for seeking health information is understandable. Vast amounts of information about medicine, including diagnosis and treatment of illness, medications, medical research and innovations, medical care providers, and related health topics are available on the internet – information provided by healthcare professionals and organizations, the traditional media, pharmaceutical companies, university researchers, and government units. On one hand, the potential of the internet as a tool for enhancing patients' ability to cope with health conditions is argued to be extraordinary.[75,76] It supports the accumulation of information by individuals and the dissemination of information. Social media such as Facebook, Twitter, YouTube, and online support groups are becoming more and more important as sources of health information.[77]

The internet has also become a commercial force in healthcare. For example, while traditional broadcast media may not be allowed to carry DTCA in countries outside the US and New Zealand, information about prescription medications, including promotional communications, is today available to consumers everywhere via the internet. Through social networking tools such as Facebook pages, Twitter accounts, YouTube channels, blogs, and corporate webpages, companies have multiple new online marketing opportunities beyond any geographic borders.[78] Beyond commercial interests, the absence of any regulation makes it straightforward for any group or individual to post whatever they want related to health. As a result, while the public has greater access than ever to health information, the quality of information available to consumers is more variable; hence consumers are increasingly vulnerable to exposure to misleading information. Thus, the internet has complicated the problem of providing information to health consumers and patients.

Misinformation on the Internet

The potential for medical misinformation on the internet was recognized early in its development. By 1998, dietitians were called to evaluate websites to find and expose quackery and fraud.[79] Another 1998 study examined the first 300 references identified in an internet search on management of acute gastroenteritis in young children; 60 of the documents retrieved were from traditional medical sources, and only 12 conformed to the current American Academy of Pediatrics recommendations. Thus, not only was fraudulent information appearing on the internet, even legitimate sources could be presenting inaccurate information. The problem has only grown. While information of questionable quality can and has appeared in many traditional media and spread through social groups, the problem is magnified by the internet because the cost of production is low and reach can be wide.[80,81] 'Context deficit' can exacerbate problems for the reader – lack of indicators that the information is meant for professionals or particular types of patients rather than general readers increasing potential misinterpretation or misapplication, easily skipped 'fine print' pages containing disclaimers, anonymity of author-ship, and unclear source materials, for example, reliance on personal experi-ence rather than clinical data.

Even predating social media, information distributed through the internet was problematic. In a 1994 study of an online forum (bulletin board) devoted to arm and hand pain due to repetitive use, 1,658 messages were posted by 313 participants over a five-month period.[82] Only 5% of the messages were written by healthcare providers; the great majority came from affected persons. Over half concerned medical topics, and of those, 70% were from participants without professional training, with much of the advice based on personal experience. Today, social media such as Twitter and Facebook are heavily contaminated by misinformation. A recent review found that in 69 studies published between 2013 and 2019, misinformation is particularly prevalent in the domains of vaccination, smoking (e-cigarettes and hookahs), and drug use (particularly opioids and cannabis).[83]

Outside of highly constrained domains, people are exposed to information that is incomplete (e.g., advertising for prescription medications), of question-able relevance (e.g., testimonials from friends and social media), or simply wrong (e.g., anti-vaxxer websites). The internet has enabled direct consumer access to vast amounts of health information, and while online patient decision support aids abound,[41,84] 2/3 of searches for health information on the internet start from a general-purpose search engine such as Google.[85,86] Unlike profes-sionally managed programs, search engines provide little guidance about the integrity of the links they provide or the quality of information that can be found under these links. Different links often provide conflicting viewpoints on what information is important and how judgements and decisions should be made.[87,88] In political debate, such variety might be seen as a virtue, but when it comes to health information, this lack of structure can be a curse. For a person searching the internet for health information using a general search engine, assumptions of veracity, accuracy, and relevance of the accessed information are almost certainly heroic.

To understand the impact and implications of this misinformation, we begin by considering in the next section the nature of knowledge and the character of misinformation. Then we explore in Section 3 psychological processes that help to explain individual acceptance and persistence of misinformation.

Beyond access, consumer acceptance of internet information can exacerbate the problem. Often, health consumers accept internet information uncritically, particularly when it aligns with their prior views and preferences (confirmation bias), failing to consider the quality of websites in terms of the accuracy and relevance of the presented information.[89,90] As a result, information of dubious quality is accessed, accepted, and used by consumers.[91,92] This misinformation damages trust between patient and physician as well as between the public and the public health system. As a result, these incorrect and dangerous claims, as well as false conspiracy theories, pose serious public health threats.[6,93] Before these threats can be addressed, it is necessary to understand how and why people adopt dubious claims and incorrect information, and why such beliefs are difficult to dislodge and correct.[94]

2 What Does It Mean to Be Misinformed?

While it is easy to bemoan the widespread promulgation of misinformation, it is more challenging to clarify what constitutes misinformation. Few would doubt that the information used in medical decision-making must be of high quality. Typically, quality of information refers to the empirical evidence supporting it. The GRADE (grading of recommendations, assessment, development, and evaluations) approach assesses the strength of a body of evidence by considering potential confounds present, either in the design of the study (randomized trials being very strong compared to observational data) or defects in the design including bias, imprecision, inconsistency in results of different studies, and publication bias.[95] At what point, then, does a study's GRADE score (quality) become so low that its results and recommendations are no longer trustworthy for medical decision-making? Or if there is such a score, is exceeding it enough? Medical decision-making calls for more than the best available evidence. The evidence is being applied in the context of a specific patient and the physician must use clinical expertise to tailor that application to the patient's condition and needs.[96] In addition, the patient's experience, values, and goals must enter the decision-making process.[97] As a result, applying the same information could be appropriate for some patients but inappropriate for others. In other words, not all misinformation is biased or false.

It is also important to recognize that misinformation derives in part from the patient; it is the person/patient receiving information who becomes misinformed. Beyond belief in biased, false, or inapplicable information, rejection of correct and applicable information can result in the person being misinformed. Even if the information provided to the patient is, in terms of the professional's knowledge, correct and relevant, the patient must comprehend and accept it. If the patient can't understand or refuses to believe the information, they are again likely to be misinformed. This section explores the condition of being misinformed.

How Do You Know?

Before attacking the problem of misinformation, it is important to consider what it means for a person to know something, because this provides a basis for considering how things go wrong. The debate over the nature of knowledge is venerable. Plato held that knowledge builds on truth-entailing belief, but belief alone does not constitute knowing; that requires, in addition, explanation or justification – understanding why the belief is true. Aristotle argued that, because the explanation is itself a belief, Plato's position leads to a problem of infinite regress for the explanation. For Plato, the regress ends with innate knowledge, known from birth, that is not open to challenge. Aristotle rejects this as well, arguing against the possibility of innate knowledge. Aristotle takes a different approach – proposing instead that knowledge requires explanation in terms of four 'causes' – material, formal, efficient, and final, that is, what it's made of, how it is organized, what is responsible for its organization, and its purpose or function. Aristotle offers the example of a statue of Hercules – made of bronze, in the form of Hercules, constructed by a sculptor, built to honour Hercules. Holding these linked beliefs about the statue means it is fully understood – *ergo* known. Both Plato and Aristotle take as a starting point knowledge as belief in something that is true so knowledge has a normative vision – if we know something, we *should* be able to justify its truth.

This underlying tenet has been attacked in both ancient and recent times by sceptical arguments (how can you ever know that something is true?), and arguments over the nature of knowledge remain active today. Most current analyses accept that complete verification of knowledge is not possible, so that knowledge must be accepted as fallible.[98] Even direct observation could be wrong as in the case of mistaken eyewitness accounts in legal cases. From a normative perspective, since we may be wrong, we can't claim to know something in the sense of Plato and Aristotle. Nevertheless, their basic structure of knowledge is still prominent; saying a person knows something means at least that the person holds a belief to be correct and justified.[99] To hold a belief means that the person is certain that it is correct, and being justified in that belief means there is a good reason for believing it to be correct. This view highlights two issues. First, what does it mean to be certain that a belief is correct? Hunt suggests a prominent view is that a belief could qualify as knowledge so long as one is 'certain enough so that he/she will use the knowledge to make decisions, solve problems and select/execute actions'[99] (p. 104). This does not mean, however, that the belief is in some external objective sense true. Again, knowledge is fallible and must be defended – that is, justified, which raises the second criterion.

Knowledge: Fallible But Justified

Justification, too, is a long-contested epistemological issue. Of interest here, however, is the point that knowledge requires a reason, which suggests more generally that a belief doesn't stand alone. Knowledge is contextual – meaning and evaluation of new knowledge are built on a background of pre-existing knowledge.[98] As a basis for justification, there must be a link between the background and new knowledge. Aristotle proposed association as that link and proposed four types – contiguity in space and time, similarity, contrast, and frequency. When events are noted as close together spatially or temporally, when they appear similar with or notably different from each other, or when they co-occur frequently, the association can form the basis for learning. In a sense, the association helps us make sense of or understand the new phenomenon. More recently, Thagard considered the problem of making sense of things we encounter like texts, people, or events and argued that we construct an interpretation that fits the available information and choose that interpretation that fits best.[100] He suggests that coherence arises from relations among elements (representations) of things. Some relations increase coherence, such as association, deduction, and facilitation; others decrease coherence, like inconsistency, incompatibility, and negative association. The best interpretation is one that is most coherent. Haack proposes that a belief is embedded in (coherent with) a network of other beliefs as well as supported by (founded on) direct experiences. She likens her 'foundherentist' view to the support for an entry in a crossword puzzle.[101] The entry (piece of knowledge) is consistent with the intersecting entries in the puzzle (other pieces of knowledge) forming a coherent structure, and consistent with (supported by) its clue, which Haack equates to experience. These characteristics, she argues, provide justification for the belief.

The role of this networked pre-existing knowledge in treating new information can be seen in examples like the physician's diagnosis of disease in a patient. A patient presents with difficulty breathing and crackling sounds when listening to the lungs, and a chest X-ray reveals opacity. The differential diagnosis (plausible explanations) includes viral pneumonia, bacterial pneumonia, and lung cancer. The patient reports further that the onset of breathing difficulty was abrupt and accompanied by a high fever. The sudden onset of symptoms makes cancer less likely, and the presence of opacity on chest X-ray favours a bacterial over a viral source, so the physician diagnoses bacterial pneumonia as the best explanation of the patient's symptoms. In this vignette, the physician's expertise (her background) in terms of both knowledge of diseases and experience with a range of cases (thus variation in presentation, treatment, and outcome) enables her to claim justified belief in her diagnosis – what we could call knowledge. Clearly, this inferential process leans heavily on the physician's background knowledge and diagnostic skill. The process by which a physician analyses a case (new information) to reach a diagnosis has been characterized as abduction or, more specifically, inference to the best explanation.[102]

Abduction is not limited to expert analysis. Douven suggests it is ubiquitous and a regular feature of everyday judgement.[102] He gives as an example a vignette where you hear of two friends who have fought and ended their friendship. Yet some time later, you hear they were seen jogging together. You conclude that they must have made up. The basis of your conclusion is that this is the most likely explanation (among any others that might come to mind). However, it is likely that you draw on other things you know about the friends, for example, neither tends to hold a grudge. Like the physician, you are using available data, coupled with your understanding of the context, to make a justified inference regarding the best (most likely) explanation. Notice that abductive inference is not proof. A physician's diagnostic inference might lead her to call for more tests to provide more conclusive evidence for a final diagnosis. Of course, even experts like physicians can make mistakes – applying their best judgement and medical expertise to the signs and symptoms of a particular patient's case but reaching the wrong conclusion (diagnosis or treatment). Certainly, you could be mistaken in concluding the friends made up.

This possibility of error doesn't destroy our search for confidence in knowledge, but accepting the fallibility of knowledge changes the way it is envisioned. The focus turns from a normative goal of truth to a pragmatic concern for knowledge as a strong working hypothesis. It is well supported by preexisting knowledge (allied beliefs and empirical evidence), and major inconsistent claims have been found to be implausible. While it could still be wrong, it is accepted in the absence of a compelling challenge. Popper argues that this is how science advances – through falsification.[103] A theory is accepted provisionally as one that explains phenomena of interest and has not yet been falsified. If the theory is later found wanting, a new theory may be required. From the history of science, a vivid example often discussed is the case of Newtonian physics, whose predictions regarding the motions of objects from apples to planets were supported by innumerable observations and experiments.

Yet, Newton's analysis was ultimately found to be wrong (albeit an extraordinarily successful approximation in everyday contexts) and Einstein's theory of relativity took its place as the best explanation based significantly on a famous demonstration by Arthur Eddington that light was bent by the sun. Yet even today, questions remain as to whether the theory of relativity is somehow flawed, and experiments are conducted seeking evidence for flaws or phenomena the theory can't explain. Similarly, in medicine, tests are often performed to 'rule out' possible diagnoses. Again, given the fallibility of knowledge, it is as important to rule out wrong answers as it is to link evidence favouring the answer we think is right.

Understanding: Building on the Background

Understanding and making use of new information relies on networked pre-existing or background knowledge. This background is central. When people interact with the world, they don't just sense it (see, feel, smell, etc.); they interpret it using their background knowledge. This is how people come to understand things they encounter.[104] In fact, some argue that people do more than understand; they construct the things they encounter by adopting a frame of reference.[105] A diagnosis of hypertension may mean very different things to a doctor versus a patient. For the physician, training and experience frame hypertension as a significant medical problem that increases the risk of future catastrophic events like a heart attack or stroke, so it needs to be addressed. For the patient, hypertension is invisible. It has no symptoms, and the patient, given his experiences, sees himself as healthy. As such, he might discount the seriousness of the condition and the urgency for treatment. Moreover, the side effects of some medications are uncomfortable – why make yourself feel sick?

The frame of reference arises from a background far beyond the particulars of the diagnosis. It is a function of experience, culture, values, attitudes, and other social influences. For someone raised in a Western European tradition, ginger is a slightly exotic spice. For someone raised in an Asian, particularly Chinese tradition, ginger is also a medicine useful for the treatment of a range of health problems, including nausea and vomiting, migraine, and arthritis.[106] The background, then, is implicated in activities as basic as making sense and understanding new information and applied to further uses like judgement (medical diagnosis), decision (whether or not to call the doctor), and forecasting (my sprained ankle will take two weeks to recover). It isn't possible to enumerate the components of one's background, but there are some hints as to how it is constituted.

While background knowledge certainly includes pre-existing information about the world, the example of abduction suggests that it includes something more. Gilbert Ryle[107] drew an important distinction between 'know-that' (propositional knowledge) and 'know-how' (non-propositional knowledge). Propositional knowledge is what one might typically think of as knowledge. It is presented in statements that can be examined and analysed to see whether they should be accepted or believed. The propositional structure is central: knowledge means to know something about something. Whoever claims to know something is thereby stating their belief that something specific is or is not the case.

Non-propositional knowledge includes abilities, skills, and competences, as well as practical knowledge and experience. This type of knowledge is important in allowing us to use (understand, interpret, evaluate, and apply) propositional knowledge. In concert, the two types of knowledge enable access to a certain area of reality. In contrast to propositional knowledge, however, non-propositional knowledge can neither be described by its related-ness to a specific object nor can it be adequately objectified. Even if one can make statements about a particular ability or skill, the content of that compe-tence can never be fully presented in statements and communicated to another. How an experienced doctor reaches his diagnosis, for example, cannot be described or specified in every detail, and certainly not in enough detail to allow a novice to diagnose new cases. The skills involved are developed through training and experience and are not simply the sum of propositional knowledge. In addition, such non-propositional knowledge is inherent to a person in a different way than is the case with propositional knowledge. It cannot simply be adopted; it can only be acquired by oneself, which explains the limited ability to communicate it. Try, for example, to explain how you are able to read this text.

Non-propositional knowledge is essential for the acquisition of new information and knowledge. How else could one assimilate new information? Searle identifies key functions of the background: enabling linguistic and perceptual interpretation, structuring consciousness (in a sense similar to that suggested by Thagard and Haack), assigning categories to objects and narrative meaning to sequences of experiences, and thereby setting up conditional expectations regarding interaction with the objects and other experiences, and mobilizing motivational and behavioural dispositions.[108,109] In this way, the background enables meaning to be attached to new information.

Subjectivity

People learn about new things in many ways. Sometimes they observe something new directly. For example, walking down the street, you see a sign in a shop window saying a health clinic will be opening soon. Or they might experience it – their doctor is on an extended trip and they are seen by a *locum tenens* physician taking her place for a period of time. However, much of what we learn is not direct, but things we are exposed to via communication. We learn about health from TV news and advertising, friends and neighbours, and social media. When we experience a health problem, we consult the internet or a health professional like a physician, therapist, or pharmacist. This means that much of our knowledge is socially constructed. Other people are providing us with information and telling us what it means – how to interpret and understand it, that is, develop knowledge about it.

This social aspect of knowledge adds a new complexity to what we can claim to know. Searle proposes some clarifying distinctions.[108] He first notes our everyday or commonsense distinction between objective and subjective knowledge. He terms this epistemic, relating to statements like 'The carrot in my refrigerator weighs fifty grams' versus statements like 'I prefer the flavour of carrots to that of broccoli'. The first statement is epistemically objective in that we can test its truth by referencing a feature of the external world, for example, the reading of a scale. The second statement is not testable in this way. It is epistemically subjective; the 'truth' of the statement lies in the judgement of the person making the claim, and like any preference statement *de gustibus non est disputandum*. One may feel strongly about preferences, believe in them, and make decisions based on them. One can also present an argument (justification) for them. However, the truth of the statement is not testable by reference to a feature of the external world.

Searle proposes an additional distinction. He argues that there are ontologically subjective and objective facts. Ontological subjectivity relates to the existence of the entity itself – the *existence* of an ontologically subjective entity is 'observer relative'. The fact that a chemist has synthesized 2-(4-isobutylphenyl) propionic acid in a laboratory is ontologically objective – the compound exists whether or not I am aware of it. On the other hand, the fact that I take ibuprofen (the pharmaceutical name for that compound) to lessen my knee pain is ontologically subjective. Ibuprofen would not be an analgesic if I were not there to experience it. In other words, the fact that ibuprofen is an effective analgesic was created by people and shared with others who accepted it. The analgesic function is certainly tied to its chemical composition, but if there were no people to experience it, ibuprofen could not be an analgesic. Thus, ibuprofen *as an analgesic* is ontologically subjective.

Much of a person's interaction with health products and services is subjective, either ontologically or epistemically (I like ibuprofen because it helps to get rid of my headache) or both. This is because we interact with them with a purpose in mind, and as such, their existence *as products* must be ontologically subjective. Ibuprofen is an analgesic because people use it as one. The shared recognition of use is significant. Among ontologically subjective facts, Searle distinguishes a class that is: (1) intentional, that is, they reflect purposes and goals, and more specifically (2) functional in an agentive sense, that is, they reflect the use of an object relative to a purpose or goal, and (3) collective, that is, they are shared by members of a relevant group. These are *social facts* – shared mental facts that relate to the function assigned to an entity to fulfil some purpose. When the pharmaceutical company Boots introduced ibuprofen in the UK as a prescription medication under the brand name Brufen, it was introduced to physicians as an effective analgesic for rheumatoid arthritis. While advertising and promotion increase awareness, they are often viewed with scepticism and suspended disbelief. As physicians gained experience with Brufen, they found it efficacious and grew to accept the advertised claim. Thus, through its marketing, Boots created the social fact that Brufen is a product effective for managing arthritic pain.

Searle proposes one further refinement of social facts. Some social facts arise from the nature of the object, for example, using ibuprofen as an analgesic. Other social facts are unrelated to an object *per se* but are created and continue to exist only because people treat them as facts. For example, a patient about to undergo a surgical procedure signs a consent form, creating a social fact called informed consent. This status is recognized by the patient, her healthcare providers, and others as a fact – that the patient understands what is to be done and states that this is acceptable. More generally, it is accepted that informed consent is expected and officially sanctioned by the government for all such procedures. Searle calls these institutional facts. Institutional facts exist because (and continue to exist only so long as) people collectively accept them.

Given social facts, then, knowledge involves more than the attainment of objective facts about the world. Moreover, even knowledge about epistemically objective facts is fallible. We can believe and provide justification for belief and make a strong case for it using our cognitive skills and pre-existing background knowledge, but we could still be wrong. With social facts, which are created and continue to exist through collective acceptance, even a direct link to objective facts may not be invoked. This doesn't mean that social facts are completely arbitrary. They can be supported by (coherent with) justifying data – for example, a consensus of expert opinion, the best available evidence, and institutional sanction. However, justification as a process is not enough to address fallibility. Lay consensus for incorrect information could result in a social fact that is not true.[110]

Using Knowledge: Applying Facts

The point of requiring that knowledge consist of justified beliefs is to increase the likelihood that knowledge is veridical. In professional discussions of health and medicine, the focus is 'the facts', which refers to information that is epistemically objective. The importance of veridical objective knowledge in the domain of health is very practical; without it, health professionals cannot provide advice that improves patients' health, and patients risk making choices that will not improve and may worsen their health. The question, of course, is how to know what information qualifies as veridical. This is one of the most important functions of non-propositional knowledge – assessing the veracity of information.

Vaccination against childhood diseases, including measles, is safe and effective in preventing serious possible complications, including lifelong disabilities. Of course, this requires a definition of 'safe and effective'. Vaccines against childhood illnesses today are 85–90% effective in preventing disease.[111] Clinical studies and epidemiological data show that serious adverse events are rare and in many cases are shown to be caused by factors unrelated to vaccination. Cases of actual adverse events due to vaccination are extremely rare. The rate of anaphylactic reaction to vaccines in general is estimated at about 1.3 per million vaccine doses.[112] To give some context, the odds of being struck by lightning – the prototypical benchmark for rare events – is 1 in 15,300 in an 80-year lifetime,[113] 85 times more likely than vaccine anaphylaxis. Based on thousands of studies of vaccine safety and efficacy, the safety of vaccines is an epistemically strongly justified fact. The vast majority of healthcare professionals form a community of belief, and government agencies like the US Food and Drug Administration lend official approval and supportive infrastructure for vaccination. All these facts provide a strong evidentiary basis for a professional to justify medical advice. Thus, given the purpose of protecting people's health, that vaccination is safe, effective, and therefore to be encouraged is an institutional fact. This network of background knowledge leads to the professional's recommendation that unless there is a specific contraindication, a person should be vaccinated – an epistemically subjective statement but again, coherent with and justified by a network of background knowledge.

The internet has given patients and consumers access to these statistics and professional advice, but it also gives them access to contrary arguments – that vaccination is neither safe nor effective. However, the evidentiary base for these arguments relies not on systematic research but anecdote, speculation, and emotional plea. The stories may be compelling in their tragedy, but they provide no systematic evidence for the purported danger of vaccination. Knowledge may be fallible, but that doesn't mean that any belief is as justified as any other. It is not enough that a child's diagnosis of autism followed a vaccination. Temporal contiguity is only one aspect of a causal link. Other possible causes must be ruled out and using far more evidence, inference made to the best explanation. In that process, a vast body of research has shown no systematic link between vaccination and autism. To provide a ground for sound judgement and decision, the network of beliefs must conform to the full range of external evidence.

Being Misinformed

In essence, being misinformed is believing in information that is not true. Given that knowledge is fallible, it is unsurprising that people could hold beliefs that are objectively untrue. The case of particular interest is reliance on new information that is objectively incorrect or inapplicable, or rejection of that which is correct and relevant, buttressed by substantial coherence of beliefs with problematic supporting evidence. Being misinformed is typically viewed as aberrant. Experts often vilify those promulgating false information and bemoan those who believe them as either mistaken or unable to sort fact from fiction. However, misinformed beliefs are often linked (justified) into a coherent worldview that is apparently consistent with a coherence mechanism of justification and difficult to dislodge.[114] In other words, being misinformed can arise from the same process (non-propositional knowledge) as being well informed.

For example, people refusing to vaccinate their children may not be responding to the objective facts about vaccination. They respond instead to a social reality built on a network of social facts, many of which are not epistemically objective facts. Because one published study, later retracted, claimed to show that childhood measles vaccination was associated with autism, a substantial number of people continue to promulgate this claim. Coupled with a background of suspicion of pharmaceutical companies (they're just in it for the money) and a romantic vision of self-reliance (I can protect my child), some parents exposed to the claim find it compelling. The claim that vaccinations are dangerous to their children's health becomes a social fact – one shared by a worldwide community of parents and which is sustained as a social fact by their continued belief. For such believers, vaccination refusal is a way to avoid rapacious Big Pharma and use common sense and experience to protect their children. The stance is not structurally incoherent; as such, the process (use of non-propositional knowledge) by which a person might reach this belief is not 'irrational'. The problem is the content. The social reality is not tied to the epistemically objective facts about vaccination but to a set of social facts based on information that is either wrong or doesn't logically provide support for the belief. That pharmaceutical companies seek profit does not mean their products are useless or dangerous and medical expertise is often needed to manage health. Still, for people in this community, the beliefs appear coherent and justified. Unfortunately, with respect to vaccination, they are misinformed and the beliefs pose dangers to both the child and the larger population. What is important to understand, then, is how and why people come to 'get it wrong'.

Evaluating Information: The Importance of Objective Facts in Health

In some domains, the links between cause and effect, and thus the criteria appropriate for evaluating claims, can be difficult to discern. In political economy, the impact of policies is often difficult to predict with any precision, and their adoption often has unintended consequences. Globalization was promoted as increasing economic efficiency (thus wealth) but grossly underestimated the dislocations for those whose jobs moved to other countries. Those defending globalization might argue that this reflects a clash of goals and that wealth creation is the greater good. Beyond such reasoned disagreements, social facts with weak justification thrive in a range of contexts. Some of the most notorious in recent years can be found in politics, where 'fake news' – a term used to cast doubt on any media coverage that disagrees with a preferred position – invites the hearer to ignore the disagreeable information regardless of the evidence, including even direct observation. When Donald Trump was inaugurated in 2017, his press secretary claimed that the audience was the largest ever, and when challenged by photographic evidence, Trump claimed the criticism to be fake news. A senior advisor described the claim as not a falsehood but an 'alternative fact'.[104] The torrent of such unsupported claims (disinformation), particularly from highly visible political commentators, lends greater legitimacy to the claims – true or false. The prevalence of alternative facts and widespread belief in them, for example, among millions of avid Trump supporters in the US, has been more broadly described as 'post-truth society'.[115] This phenomenon is ascribed at least in part to extreme political polarization in which core values and goals are in conflict among political groups; that is, the selective acceptance and interpretation of presented information is driven by a political frame of reference which, in turn, gives rise to particular goals and objectives such as justifying denial of the legitimacy of the 2020 presidential election.

One would like to think that health is different from politics. While people argue about what constitutes a good state or government, the idea of good health seems clearer. The WHO summarizes this idea as 'Health is a state of complete physical, mental and social well-being and not merely the absence of disease or infirmity'.[116] It is hard to imagine that less well-being and more disease would be better health objectives. In the domain of health, then, even social facts relate to actual health goals and outcomes. Accurate information about health, health promotion, and medical treatment helps to advance the goal of improving health or at least not making it worse. This feature of health information is critically important in that it makes it possible to move beyond differences of opinion. In measuring health knowledge, for example, we can appeal to expert consensus to distinguish between fact and fiction so that it is meaningful to say that the better a person's ability to make this distinction – identify correct statements as correct and incorrect statements as incorrect – the greater the person's health knowledge.

However, thinking about health doesn't take place in a vacuum; it is embedded in a larger background that can distort it. Recent controversies over the management of Covid-19 highlight the importance of this feature of health knowledge. With Covid-19, the ground (background) and perspective of discussion shifted for many from health to politics. Those arguing against mandated wearing of masks, social distancing, and vaccination positioned the policies as government intrusion attacking personal choice. Opposing or refusing to comply with such mandates was seen as 'standing up to' government encroachment on personal freedom. This shifted the focus away from objective health knowledge to subjective political opinion and social facts about government, where charges and countercharges of fake news and alternative facts held sway and choices could be seen as serving more important goals and information inconsistent with those goals could be rejected.

The foregoing discussion of knowledge might suggest a very deliberate and probative approach to accepting new information. In everyday life, we do not test our explanations rigorously. We make an observation (I have a migraine) or an inference (My headache is a migraine because it is too severe to be something else) and act on it. Rarely do we consider whether we might be mistaken about the headache and generate and test alternative explanations for it. Much of the time, we are likely to treat our knowledge as verified and sufficient and use it that way. Only if challenged or when we feel we don't know enough are we likely to consider whether we could be wrong. The next section elaborates on the ways this can lead people to be misinformed.

3 Patterns of Health Knowledge Failure

This section situates being misinformed as a type of knowledge failure – how people come to 'get it wrong'. First, distinguishing three types of knowledge failure – ignorance, low literacy, and misinformation – helps to specify the specific failures that characterize being misinformed. The discussion then turns to an examination of various factors that contribute to an individual's becoming misinformed about medicine and health (especially their own health), highlighting the impact of cognitive heuristics and the role of motivation. This discussion provides a basis for consideration in the next section of how people have sought to prevent and correct misinformation.

Once again, it is important to remember that the information environment itself is a major factor in consumer and patient misunderstanding. From the 'puffery' (expansive claims) of advertising messages to the outright inaccuracies posted online or otherwise published, consumers seeking health information are inundated with questionable as well as accurate information. Assembling and making sense of this jumble is challenging, and the strategies that consumers use can lead them to erroneous beliefs and judgements.

Knowledge Failures

When considering how someone can get something wrong, it is important to distinguish three types of knowledge failure – ignorance, low literacy, and misinformation. The first case of knowledge failure is being uninformed, which can arise from the most obvious of reasons – simple lack of awareness or disinterest. If an issue is of little relevance or interest, a person has little motivation to attend to information about it. Someone who has never experienced severe back pain is likely to know little about the risks and benefits of medical versus surgical interventions for it. Even if an issue is potentially important (e.g., complex social issues such as energy policy and economic policy), ignorance can lead to avoidance of rather than search for information and to low engagement.[117] Subjectively, one who has little or no information about a topic could recognize this and be aware of their ignorance and if asked about the topic answer 'I don't know'. Those who recognize their lack of health knowledge are more likely to be open to accepting accurate information and a common strategy is to simply accept advice from credible sources like a physician or pharmacist. The central task in this case may be to get people's attention – that there is a potential problem, and the information is important. In other cases, however, should an immediate need for such information arise, people may use their general background knowledge to formulate a guess. Beyond the possibility of guessing wrong, the problem with guessing is that the person may grow overconfident of their answer and whether right or wrong form a stronger belief than is warranted,[11] which shifts the problem to one of being misinformed.

Low Literacy

A second reason for knowledge failure is inability – the problem of low literacy, particularly limited ability to read and comprehend text, which is termed functional literacy. A low-literate person could lack knowledge even if they seek to become more informed. In the domain of health, measures of functional health literacy assess a person's ability to pronounce medical words (REALM),[118] measure reading and numeracy skills by asking respondents to fill in gaps in texts (TOFHLA),[119] and answer questions about a nutrition label (Newest Vital Sign).[120] These measures tap the ability to attain the correct answer to the questions posed. Some 26% of US adults and 34% of the elderly exhibit inadequate ability to read and understand medical information, generally consistent with prevalence reported for countries in the European Union.[121] The limited ability to access and make use of health information has predictably deleterious consequences – less knowledge and comprehension of healthcare resources, lower rates of compliance with medical advice, and worse outcomes, including increased hospitalization and health costs.[12]

Researchers in health literacy realized that functional health literacy is incomplete as a basis for patient decision and action so broader conceptualizations have been developed, such as that of the US National Institutes of Health:

> **Personal health literacy** is the degree to which individuals have the ability to find, understand, and use information and services to inform health-related decisions and actions for themselves and others ... Health literacy incorporates a range of abilities: reading, comprehending, and analyzing information; decoding instructions, symbols, charts, and diagrams; weighing risks and benefits; and, ultimately, making decisions and taking an action.[122]

These abilities point to skills more complex than functional literacy. Sørensen et al. enrich the construct to include access, understanding, appraisal, and application of knowledge.[123] Such abilities depend not only on reading skills but also on background knowledge that makes health literacy contextually specific – mastery of medical information and decisions about particular medical issues so health literacy becomes context-specific.[15] Such domain-specific propositional and non-propositional knowledge is foundational to a person's ability to make sound judgements and decisions that will lead to improved health outcomes. As such, health literacy includes factual knowledge in a particular domain.[123,124] In addition, skills such as interpreting medical information by comparing data to criterial values, assessing risk, and calculating probabilities tap more demanding skills related to access, understanding, assessment, and application of medical information.[125] Lacking these skills, the person becomes more dependent on others to select and interpret information and recommend actions. Selecting the credible other then becomes an essential task, calling on, for example, 'knowledge and skills necessary to become a more mindful and sceptical news consumer'.[126]

Beyond topical specificity, the expansion of health literacy makes it personal. It invokes not only information that is immediately needed, but also the background knowledge necessary to comprehend the information in the context of the person's health, to apply the information as it pertains to the person's needs and goals, and to use the information to make personal health decisions. Low health literacy, then, refers not only to the inability to read and comprehend information, but also the inability to personalize and apply the information.

Problems due to limited health literacy have been examined in many domains. In the area of medical informed consent, lack of comprehension as well as cursory reading and limited recall are recognized as problems associated with low education and literacy.[46,127] Studies of consumer understanding of nutrition labels suggest problems using presented information such as sodium content as relating to salt, particularly among those with less education.[128] In these cases, lack of relevant information or skill using it is the foremost concern. For example, in an Australian study, pregnant women were highly motivated to consume a healthy diet and believed they were capable of doing so but actually lacked the requisite knowledge as reflected in poor adherence to recommended nutritional guidelines.[129]

Health literacy also has a subjective component – self-impressions of the ability to execute or perceived difficulty of health-related tasks. For example, the European Health Literacy Survey[130] uses scales of perceived difficulty: 'On a scale of from very easy to very difficult, how easy would you say it is to . . . .' Tasks attached to the stem include 'find information about symptoms of illnesses that concern you', 'understand what your doctor says to you', and 'judge the advantages and disadvantages of different treatment options'. Perceptual approaches to health literacy again focus on core dimensions like accessing, understanding, appraising, and applying information and provide an important bridge to empowerment – the patient's motivation to take an active role in decision. However, these perceptual measures relate imperfectly to performance-based ones. Carlson et al. report in a meta-analysis of fifty-four studies an average correlation of .37, suggesting that objective knowledge predicts only about 14% of the variation in subjective knowledge.[131]

Health literacy rests on a central assumption – that it is veridical, that is, the underlying knowledge is correct and the interpretation and application of that knowledge is sound.[15] This is necessary for people to use their literacy skills to successfully navigate contexts such as healthcare, disease prevention, and health promotion.[123] The assumption is reflected in the measurement of health literacy as the presence of the requisite skills and knowledge. The questions posed have right answers, and literacy is measured as the ability to answer correctly. The low-literate patient lacks the skills, which increases the likelihood that the patient will make mistakes and fail to make health-promoting choices.

The typical remedy proposed for limited health literacy is education – to provide the patient with relevant declarative (propositional) knowledge and procedural (non-propositional) knowledge and skills. For example, the UK Expert Patient program envisions a patient who is well informed and has access to important information about his or her chronic health condition. While a newly diagnosed diabetic might know little about the condition and its management because it was never relevant, the program makes available information filtered for accuracy and applicability, as well as professional guidance in the interpretation of that information. As the patient learns more in this program, literacy – both knowledge and skill – should increase. This expertise enables patients to take a more active role in managing their condition, improving health outcomes.[132]

Outside professionally managed programs, as discussed in Section 1, most searches for information begin with a search engine such as Google, which provides little guidance about the integrity of the websites it lists or the quality of information offered. As such, it is almost certain that some of the information will constitute misinformation. Beyond access, consumer acceptance of internet information can exacerbate the problem. Health consumers often accept internet information uncritically, particularly when it aligns with their prior views and preferences (confirmation bias), failing to consider the quality of websites in terms of the accuracy and relevance of the presented information.[89,90,133] As a result, information of dubious quality is accessed, accepted, and used.[91,92,134] As in the case of ignorance, low literacy can lead to misinformation. The broader implication is, as Hunt[99] argues, if a respondent gets it wrong (e.g., says a correct statement is incorrect), it is misleading to infer that the respondent is uncertain of the answer. It could be that the respondent believes strongly in the wrong answer. In other words, the respondent, rather than being uninformed, is misinformed.

This third type of knowledge failure – being misinformed – arises despite the person's interest in and ability to assess a health issue. The question in this case is how a person comes to 'know' things that are incorrect. Research in social psychology and the psychology of judgement and decision-making has revealed a great deal about how people attend to, perceive, and evaluate information and then use it to make judgements and decisions. In contrast to classical economic models, for example, people do not attend objectively and comprehensively to presented information and do not use the information to make consistent, informed choices. They selectively access and attend to information and process it in heuristic and biased ways. The question remains, however, why at least some of the information and conclusions drawn from it will lead to people becoming misinformed.

Becoming Misinformed

The issue raised by this question relates again to the nature of knowledge. Our analysis of knowledge to this point suggests that the goal of knowledge is truth. Even if our knowledge is fallible, we seek, to the extent possible, to ascertain the truth of propositions. However, the approach taken is often not systematic, as in the case of scientific research, but relies on memory and feelings.

If someone is highly literate in a domain – armed with a great deal of accurate information, understanding how it coheres, and aware of its implications – it is likely that evaluating new information will be guided by this prior knowledge held in memory. If new information is presented that is contrary to the person's current understanding, it is unlikely to be accepted without further examination. Even if the new information doesn't directly contradict specific known propositions, it challenges the coherence of the person's current knowledge. For an immunologist, the claim that giving multiple vaccinations at once could overload a child's immune system would be suspect because it conflicts not only with the published data but also with the immunologist's knowledge of how the immune system works. Conversely, for a layperson suspicious of vaccination safety based on stories on the internet about a controversy over vaccines and autism and a naïve conception of immunity as the body using limited resources to 'fight' infection, the claim about multiple vaccinations might well resonate. Background and feelings (anxiety about vaccination safety) would cohere with concern about overloading the immune system.

The situation just described involves being confronted with new information. The other common context in which a person encounters new information is in searching for it. The question, of course, is what guides the search for information. Much research has explored this question and found that the search can be systematic but biased. In particular, information search is prone to confirmation bias.

Confirmation Bias

Confirmation bias relates to the evidence used to reach a conclusion, such as the truth of a proposition. The bias refers to the preferential use of evidence that supports the position one already favours and discounting evidence contrary to

Figure 1 Wason Selection Task.

it. The bias is often unconscious. In the classic selection task developed by Wason, participants are shown four cards (Figure 1) and told that each has a number on one side and a letter on the other.[135]

They are then presented with a proposition: 'If a card has an A on one side then it has a 4 on the other side' and asked which cards need to be turned over to determine whether the proposition is true or false. Logically, the proposition is an implication so a disconfirming card would be one with an A and a number other than 4, which could potentially be the case for cards A and 7, that is, if card A had a 5 or card 7 had an A, the proposition would be disconfirmed. Cards B and 4 provide no information. For B, any number would be consistent with the proposition and for 4 any letter would be. Most study participants, however, choose card A or cards A and 4 suggesting they are looking at the cases that could be consistent with the proposition (confirm it) rather than seeking information that could falsify it. This tendency to seek evidence consistent with a belief or hypothesis one holds rather than disconfirming evidence is called confirmation bias.

In an extensive review, Nickerson notes 'A great deal of empirical evidence supports the idea that the confirmation bias is extensive and strong and that it appears in many guises'.[136] In information search, people tend to seek information they interpret as supporting their beliefs. People also tend to ignore or reject information they see as contrary to their beliefs or distort its interpretation to render it supportive. When asked to retrieve reasons from memory, people are more likely to recall reasons supporting their position. This approach, of course, makes it unlikely that a person will revise their beliefs or discover any shortcomings. Further, cognitive heuristics such as likelihood estimation based on availability – the ease of remembering – will reinforce these biases in judgement. These and analogous tendencies have been examined in a wide range of contexts – unwarranted optimism in gambling, social stereotyping, exacerbating hypochondria, even the credibility of fortune tellers and astrologers. The (historical) real-world dangers of confirmation bias discussed by Nickerson include jury members focusing on and preferentially recalling information consistent with a tentative verdict reached early in the trial, bias toward guilt in witch hunt trials, rationalization and justification of policies by government, theory persistence in science in the face of inconsistent data, and medicine, where either through haphazard 'testing' or chicanery, numbers of procedures like bleeding and various ineffective concoctions were promoted on the basis of 'cures' – simply biased reporting of sick people receiving the treatment recovering and suppression of cases where either the patient did not recover or recovered without treatment.

Information search today is heavily concentrated online, utilizing the internet and social media. In the domain of health, confirmation bias has been found to affect internet information search.[137,138] People tend to construct web searches that will generate results that include information consistent with current beliefs and are more likely to click on search results that appear consistent, which strengthens those beliefs – an effect described as reinforcing spirals[139] and in the case of social media, a homogeneity of views termed an 'echo chamber'.[140]

One suggestion is that this search behaviour is another consequence of low health literacy. In some cases, increased health literacy appears to help. In one study in Japan, those with lower health literacy appear to be affected by confirmation bias more than those with higher health literacy.[141] In that study, participants were first queried about the safety of genetically modified foods (negative, neutral, or positive) and their level of health literacy measured. Among those with low health literacy, those in the negative group clicked on fewer pages conflicting with their views than those in the neutral group. They also spent less time reviewing the list of results and clicked on higher-ranked webpages (reflecting shallower search). Those with high health literacy reversed this pattern, with those in the negative group clicking on more pages inconsistent with their views than those in the neutral group. However, other studies suggest that confirmation bias can persist even with high health literacy. For example, in a study of vaccination information in the Netherlands, among those with negative beliefs toward vaccination, health literacy had no influence on perceived credibility and usefulness of vaccination information.[142]

The Problem of Overconfidence

One characteristic of the homogeneous information generated by confirmation bias is the lack of dissonant feedback. This gives rise to the problem of unknown unknowns. Dunning discusses the twofold nature of this problem in task performance.[11] First, of course, lack of expertise degrades performance. Second, the respondent often will be unaware of this lack of expertise because 'evaluating the correctness of one's (or anyone else's) response draws upon the exact same expertise that is necessary in choosing the correct response in the first place' (p. 261). As a result, they are unaware of their lack of expertise – an example of an unknown unknown. This lack of awareness has been demonstrated in a variety of settings, including text comprehension,[143] political knowledge,[144] and knowledge of clinical procedures.[145] These unknown unknowns impact self-perceptions of competence or subjective knowledge. Kruger and Dunning show that subjects (in their case students) who perform poorly on a test (lack expertise) have little sense of their lack and overestimate their performance both in absolute terms and relative to others.[146] Dunning notes two heuristic reasons for this overestimation. First, the subjects may believe they know more than they do – drawing on intuitive 'knowledge' or general impressions to derive an answer. These intuitions are often simply wrong and lead subjects to a wrong answer but a perception that their answer is rational and sound. Second, subjects may draw on a perceived false consensus – that other people have similar levels of knowledge and will perform similarly. Even the objectively worst performing quartile of subjects estimate their performance to be average or above. By contrast, high performers typically understate their performance relative to others. Dunning argues that this is due to a perception that, since the problems seem simple and straightforward, high performers assume that others experience the problems similarly.

As a result of this overestimation, one who is misinformed may feel well informed and capable of making health judgements and decisions – overconfident in their expertise. For example, anti-vaccination views can be explained as a problem of unknown unknowns – a person's overconfidence in knowledge of vaccination even though it is wrong.[147] The task of correcting misinformation can be more difficult than providing correct information. The misinformation is often consistent with the person's preferences, other beliefs (e.g., distrust of government or medical institutions), and subject to confirmation bias when exposed to new information, ignoring that which is inconsistent with the misinformed beliefs.

Empowerment and the Danger of Being Misinformed

In addition to overconfidence, the dangers of being misinformed are exacerbated by the growth of patient empowerment. This means that those who are misinformed will act on that misinformation. Both health literacy and patient empowerment have been advanced as important determinants of a range of health-related behaviours and the outcomes of patient communication and public health efforts. However, the two are often conflated in studies, and studies of one regularly either ignore or assume the other. Health literacy and patient empowerment, albeit closely interwoven, are distinct concepts and must be considered in conjunction to understand the problem of misinformation.[15]

Patient empowerment, introduced in Section 1, evolved as a consequence of the growth of respect for autonomy as a core value in medical care. In a general sense, empowerment can be viewed as a 'process by which people gain mastery over their lives'.[148] To improve the quality of their lives, people should be able and motivated to bring about changes, not only in their personal behaviour but also in their social situations and the organizations that influence their lives. From the standpoint of the individual patient, empowerment implies informed choice[14] and feelings of power, control, and greater self-esteem.[31,149] This psychological view of patient empowerment highlights the patient's desire to participate in healthcare decisions. This makes empowerment and its dimensions motivational constructs and therefore volitional. The empowered patient emerges as a person who does not passively receive information he then tries to comprehend and invariably accepts, but as someone who extracts meaning relevant to himself from proffered information and advice and chooses and enacts behaviours he concludes are appropriate to his present health situation. If empowered patients are to make choices that promote their health, they must have the required knowledge and skills, that is, health literacy.

Distinguishing Health Literacy and Empowerment

Much literature on patient empowerment has examined initiatives in which health professionals design programs that show increased self-management by patients improves their access to services, their ability to manage their disease, and their health outcomes. More generally, as stated for the British Expert Patient program, the vision is that 'many more patients with chronic diseases are well informed about their condition and medication, feel empowered in their relationship with health care professionals, and have higher self-esteem'.[132] Thus, the programs take as a goal both situational and psychological empowerment of the patient. However, the mechanics of the program rely heavily on education seeking to improve patient literacy regarding their health condition. Work on health literacy regularly includes empowerment as a goal but seems to assume that high levels of expertise will naturally lead to effective involvement in medical decisions or beneficial self-management. For too many patients, this assumption is heroic. For example, parents who refuse vaccination for their children are exercising empowerment but it is based on information that is wrong or unrelated to vaccination. The problem of a misinformed and empowered patient is that he or she could well make dangerous choices.[15] At the other extreme is the highly literate patient lacking in psychological empowerment who remains highly dependent on health professionals despite

		Health literacy		
		Low	Misinformed	High
Psychological empowerment	High	Error-prone patient	Dangerous self-manager	Effective self-manager
	Low	High-needs patient	Questioning/ argumentative patient	Needlessly dependent patient

Figure 2 Health Literacy, Empowerment, and Patient Behaviour.

their apparent ability to make well-informed decisions for themselves. Thus, health literacy and empowerment are distinct and health outcomes will depend on both (Figure 2).

The idealized vision of advocates of both improved health literacy and patient empowerment is to move people from the lower and left cells of the figure to the upper right one – helping patients to become more effective self-managers of their health, using healthcare resources appropriately to optimize their health outcomes. Self-management doesn't mean they have to do it on their own. Effective self-management also includes the use of available resources like educational programs and expert advice. Making such resources available is an important part of seeking to advance health literacy and effective self-management. Nevertheless, as suggested by the examples above, a central problem in a health management context may lie in the mismatch of literacy and empowerment, so that any intervention must be sensitive to the impact of the other construct.

Bounding Literacy and Empowerment

Accepting that the patient needs to know more raises the question of what information makes a person health literate. The expanded visions of health literacy discussed earlier involve the patient assessing the meaning of information, analysing it relative to a health issue, and using that analysis to participate in health decisions. Literacy programs are directed at patients lacking in knowledge and skills, so the programs proceed from a vision that more is better. Similarly, analyses of patient empowerment often are responding to the vestiges of paternalism and, as a result, advocate for greater empowerment. It is important to remember, however, that self-management need not mean completely autonomous decision-making. Nor does health literacy mean that patients gain the expertise of a physician or even some sort of pale shadow of one. The patient has unique knowledge of the symptoms, character, and consequences of his or her health problems, that is, the experience of the health problems. This knowledge needs to be communicated to the health professionals so that they can bring their expertise to bear. As noted in Section 1, empowered care becomes a constrained collaboration.

In other words, patient literacy and empowerment must be bounded. Even an empowered patient should not be diagnosing and treating himself. The literate patient not only has knowledge but also has a sense of the limits of that knowledge and when to seek help. In the expanded literacy framework, literacy could enable the patient to make judgements about when it is advisable to seek expert advice from a health professional, find the appropriate one, explain the health problem and personal concerns that made the consultation necessary, and interpret the professional's guidance as it relates to their own health. Effective self-managing patients are active in their healthcare decisions, but also making appropriate use of available professional advice and support.

When this goes wrong because of misinformation, the intersection of health literacy, patient empowerment, and misinformation creates a complex problem for health professionals and public policy managers in seeking to convince patients to make healthy choices. This is the challenge considered in the next section.

4 Addressing Knowledge Failures

Being uninformed and being misinformed can both lead to flawed judgements and decisions resulting in negative outcomes, but they are substantially different.[7,150,151] Being uninformed increases the likelihood of mistakes, but being misinformed makes these errors systematic. In light of this difference, the remedies for these two knowledge failures differ. The answer traditionally posed to address the uninformed is education – teaching people what they need to know about their health to enhance their ability to make good choices. Beyond reading and numeracy, literacy programs in specific areas seek to improve knowledge and skills to make choices that enhance good outcomes in health, either through training of individuals or tailoring communications to them. Misinformation, on the other hand, involves the much more challenging task of correcting inaccurate beliefs and persuading the person that the correction is appropriate, and often, inducing them to reframe the issue so that the corrected information is coherent with their background.

Addressing Ignorance: Improving Health Literacy

Consumers with low health literacy capabilities will be less capable in using veridical information they face; therefore, their decisions will be less beneficial or even detrimental to their health. Improving health literacy takes as a goal not just the ability to read and comprehend health communications, but to access and hold veridical – accurate and relevant – health information and to use this information to make decisions beneficial to their health. Moreover, avoiding detrimental health decisions when faced with erroneous information requires that the consumer recognize specific health information as inaccurate or irrelevant. These judgements require abilities beyond basic understanding and interpretation. To complicate things further, there is a subjective meta-level of thinking concerned with one's own qualification to pass judgement on the veridicality of health information. One can be confident about one's ability to make that judgement or a decision related to it, or one can be sceptical of one's capabilities in this respect.

Health literacy then invokes four consumer abilities:

1. To access health information.
2. To understand, process, and interpret health information.
3. To evaluate the accuracy and relevance of the health information.
4. To assess the sufficiency of one's own knowledge (item 1 above) and abilities (items 2 and 3 above) to make a decision.

Classic health literacy research has focused on capability 2, but if health literacy is to improve a person's ability to make health decisions, all four capabilities are essential. There is also a move from objective to subjective approaches in the order of the four levels. The actual accuracy of information a person accesses is an objective question. The consumer's performance in understanding the information can be imagined to be approached by objective as well as by subjective approaches – not only understanding correctly but feeling that one understands. Assessing relevance is necessarily subjective because it relates to the person's goals, and assessing sufficiency is highly subjective. Finally, even if an external observer might make an objective assessment of the person's knowledge and skill as it relates to a domain, the person's willingness to make independent decisions is highly subjective. This subjectivity is important as it links literacy skills to motivation and willingness to participate in health decisions.

The task of addressing ignorance then extends well beyond addressing capability 1 by providing accurate information. In many cases, for example, the problem is one of convincing someone that there is a problem in the first place – an aspect of capabilities 2 and 3. Although the patient's blood pressure is elevated, he feels fine. Indeed, some of the medications prescribed to control blood pressure can have side effects that make the patient feel worse. At a minimum, then, the patient must be educated about the serious health risks posed by hypertension and the benefits of controlling it, how it can be controlled, the costs (not only financial but also possible side effects and inconvenience), and how to track the results, for example, monitoring blood pressure.

The patient needs to understand the problem and its potential solution, but also why it matters and that managing their hypertension gives them the ability to control a health problem. As a result of this education, the patient is both informed (accurately) and provided with the skill (how to monitor blood pressure) and tools (medications) to manage their hypertension. As discussed earlier, people seek coherent information and a context in which the information makes sense. The goal of an educational program must be to provide a coherent story that informs and explains the patient's health problem and its solution.

This can be challenging in situations where providing information makes the patient's perception of their health worse. Being told that the aches and pains they are experiencing are not just ageing but rheumatoid arthritis is likely devastating. Indeed, in the past, it was a recommended practice not to tell the diagnosis to patients who the physician thought would react with 'emotional instability'.[152] As that is no longer an accepted practice, a literature has developed around delivering bad news. With respect to cancer, for example, almost all patients want to know they have the disease and their prognosis, and as many as two-thirds want to participate in treatment decisions.[153] At the same time, patients want the delivery of that information to be tailored to their situation. This presents a complex task for the physician. As one example, the SPIKES approach for oncologists[154] suggests a process: (1) *setting up* the interview (e.g., providing a private space), (2) assessing the patient's *perception* of their health problem and what they have already been told about it, (3) obtaining the patient's *invitation*, determining how much the patient wants to know right now and what should be postponed for a later discussion, (4) delivering, beginning with a warning of the bad news to come, the information (*knowledge*), tailoring vocabulary to the patient's ability and breaking down the information into manageable chunks, (5) recognizing the difficulty for the patient and responding to their *emotions* with empathy, and (6) discussing a treatment *strategy* if the patient is ready to do so involving the patient in a shared decision process. Not only are such approaches designed to increase patient comfort, but they also increase patient satisfaction with the physician and trust in provided information and treatment recommendations. Patient-centred approaches to information provision reflect nuanced approaches to increasing patient health literacy, addressing all four capabilities. In the case of cancer, for example, patient-centred discussion of treatment options (including no treatment) can enable patients to consider trade-offs of longevity versus quality of life and make reasoned choices about the acceptability of treatments. While autonomous patient self-management is an unlikely goal in cancer, for other chronic health conditions, the goal of patient education may well be substantial self-management as is common for diabetes and asthma. In short, patient-centred approaches seek to address both objective and subjective information needs to improve both health literacy and empowerment.

The issue of ignorance may seem natural in the case of a novel health problem or diagnosis. However, in the broader health context, it is likely to be unusual. For many, if not most, health problems and needs, people already have prior exposure and knowledge, and often have opinions. When their exposure is biased or their knowledge is wrong, the problem is no longer being ignorant but being misinformed.

'Falling For' Misinformation

When presented with new information, prior knowledge serves as an important reference in deciding how to respond. To judge the truth of a novel statement, checking its consistency with prior knowledge is natural.[155] Statements that are consistent with other information in memory are more likely to be accepted as true. Information that is inconsistent with prior knowledge is more difficult to process and can cue a negative affective response.[156] Of course, if the bases of the 'truth' of prior knowledge are unreliable, then consistency with memory can result in incorrect judgements about the truth of the new information, which in turn impacts decisions. A classic example was the failure of a public health campaign in a Peruvian village to encourage villagers to boil water to prevent disease. The villagers, for the most part, believed that cooked water was associated with illness so that boiling water would make them sick.[157] Even children found the idea of boiled water disgusting. The suggestion was inconsistent with the villagers' conception of hot and cold water – the social fact that cold water was for healthy people and hot water for the sick, and even after three years of effort, adoption of the program was limited.

Cognition: The Impact of Heuristic Processing

People are not aware of being misinformed; they believe their information is true. The problem is that their bases for judging truth are unreliable.[155] In the face of an overwhelming amount of information, people rely on mental short-cuts to make judgements about what to believe and what information to use in making judgements. Tversky and Kahneman proposed that these shortcuts take the form of heuristics – easier and faster algorithms for making judgements.[158] They showed that ease of generating examples increased judgements of frequency – termed the availability heuristic, and that featural similarity predicted judgements of category membership – the representativeness heuristic. With respect to judgements of truth, people likewise unthinkingly employ fast and easy heuristics. One important heuristic for assessing truth is reliance on a feeling of comfort with the content. Coherence with information in memory is an important basis for such feeling. However, comfort can be enhanced by mechanisms seemingly unrelated to the content. For example, repeated exposure to claims makes them familiar and more likely to be accepted as true – an effect called illusory truth.[159] This is why advertising campaigns employ repeated presentations of messages. People are more likely to be exposed to them and repeated exposure increases acceptance of the messages. It is also why the spread of information on social media, creating repetitive exposure, is influential even in the case of retweets of messages not opened. Just repeated exposure to a headline can make an impact on perception of truth.

Repetition works because it makes things more likely to be recalled (available). It also makes it easier to recognize and process that information when presented again – an effect called fluency. Repetition is not the only route to fluency.[155,156] Simply making statements easier to read using a more readable font, higher colour contrast, or more readable handwriting increases fluency compared to a font that is difficult to read. Neither repetition nor ease of reading relates to the truth of the statement, so fluency is not a reliable indicator of a statement's veracity. Yet, fluency acts as a strong cue for judgements of truth – the ease of accessing fluent information makes individuals feel it is (should be, must be) true. Repeated presentation of false information increases ratings of truth. Even when respondents know the information is not true, they may give increased truth ratings for repeated false statements apparently relying on fluency rather than checking their knowledge.[160] Fluency can even stand in for coherence of information because inconsistency with prior knowledge disrupts the processing of the new information, decreasing fluency. Recalling the confirmation bias discussed in Section 3, people rely on confirmation to assess truth. Rather than 'sifting the evidence' in search of contradiction to evaluate information, they can rely on fluency. Because fluency makes information 'feel' right, it can also feel coherent, thus more likely to be true.

Heuristic processing of information also has a social component. For example, particularly when people don't process information extensively, credibility of information is signalled by the credibility of the source. Studies of cognitive response to persuasion have long recognized the importance of a credible source for the acceptance of persuasive messages. Credibility can be inferred from actually informative characteristics, such as evidence of expertise like educational attainment and important achievements, but it can also be inferred from characteristics that are not really related to expertise, such as familiarity and attractiveness.[161] The use of celebrities to promote products in advertising draws on their notoriety as a cue to credibility. The actor or athlete wearing a brand of watch actually offers little information beyond their own attractiveness but can still convey to fans a perception of quality, style, and exclusivity.

A related cue is perceived acceptance of the information by others.[162] Widespread acceptance, particularly among in-group members or people viewed as similar, promotes information acceptance. Homophily is a powerful cue. 'People like me' are naturally credible, and when a lot of them endorse information, it is more likely to be accepted. The problem again is that an inference of widespread acceptance is affected by factors other than actual consensus.[156] Repeated exposure to information, even from the same person, increases belief in its accuracy. An account that appears in multiple social media posts makes readers more confident of the account's accuracy, even if it is based on the same source and even the same interview with that source. Thus, many of the cues people use to assess the veracity of information – fluency, availability, and source credibility – are influenced by factors other than information content. As a result, they can lead to erroneous judgements, and they also create opportunities for persuasive manipulation.

Affect: The Impact of Emotions

The heuristics discussed focus on cognitive processes. Another important influence on judgement and decision-making is affect, particularly emotions.[163,164] One prominent view of this process is the appraisal tendency framework, which holds that 'an emotion, once activated, can trigger a cognitive predisposition to assess future events in line with the central appraisal dimensions that triggered the emotion' (p. 805).[163] The framework incorporates emotional appraisals beyond valence. Fear and anger, for example, both have a negative valence but elicit different responses because they involve other appraisals such as certainty (predictability), individual control, and others' responsibility. Anger is high in all three of these dimensions while fear is low in certainty and individual control and medium in others' responsibility. As a result, anger promotes a vision of control, leading to a perception of lower risk and riskier choices. Fear, on the other hand, promotes a perceived lack of predictability and control, leading to a perception of higher risk and a choice of less risky options.

Some emotions are elicited by the judgement or decision at hand. Such integral emotions are influential. For example, faced with a decision about treatment of cancer, the fear induced by the diagnosis itself can lead to selecting options perceived to be safer. This is also consistent with cuing of a prevention mindset as suggested in research on regulatory focus,[165] where focus on preventing negative outcomes leads to choosing lower risk options. On the other hand, a patient diagnosed with mesothelioma (a type of lung cancer) associated with exposure to asbestos might well be angry at his employer because he was likely exposed on the job and, as a result, seek more aggressive treatment even if it involved greater risk. Whether this effect of emotion contributes optimally to improving the patient's health is not certain. It is unclear whether choosing a treatment that has a greater potential for longer remission but greater risk of disability is the best choice for quality of life.

Returning to the theme of misinformation, incidental emotions unrelated to the decision at hand can also influence decision-making. Emotions cued by an unrelated newspaper article or even the weather (a sunny versus rainy day) can influence decision-making, particularly when the decision is complex, novel, or unanticipated.[229,230] This, once again, means that judgement and decision may be influenced by emotional responses that have little bearing on the issue at hand. It also once again opens the door for manipulation; by inducing feelings, a decision-maker can be nudged toward different choices. If one is angered by an internet blog and that anger carries over to a healthcare deliberation, it could foster greater risk-taking. A patient choosing such a treatment might suffer later regret about the decision, viewing it as an error.

The problem posed by the effects of incidental and unrelated sources of fluency, false consensus (the erroneous perception that others share my views), and affect is that they can give rise to a mistaken self-perception of literacy. In terms of the literacy skills noted earlier, these effects degrade the person's ability to evaluate the accuracy and relevance of information. In addition, biases toward confirmation and overconfidence combined with these effects lead people to overestimate the sufficiency of their abilities and knowledge as bases for making a decision. Correcting these problems presents challenges quite different from the tasks of educating the uninformed.

Persisting in Being Misinformed

A person who is presented with information to correct misinformation will meet the new information like any other and accept or reject it using the same processes. As such, when someone is misinformed, the task of correcting errors is challenging.[166] Previous sections discussed the characteristics of the information environment, the nature of knowledge, and the varieties of knowledge failures. All of these filter through an information evaluation process, which increases the difficulty of effectively changing people's minds about misinformation.

Continued Exposure: The Information Environment

As the information environment has evolved, so too has the opportunity to spread misinformation. Because the internet is relatively unfiltered for accuracy, when people search for information about a health problem, they are likely to encounter inaccurate as well as accurate information and the presentation of misinformation often mimics that of accurate information from authoritative sources. Unproven or disproven cures are promoted using testimonials from people with advanced degrees (MD or Ph.D.) or simply claiming the title 'Doctor', seeking credibility. Testimonials from success stories suggest the cure works for 'regular' people suggesting widespread utility (social consensus). A story of the inventor's heroic struggle to provide a miraculous cure despite harassment from moneyed corporate interests and corrupt government agencies might offer a distorted or even fictitious narrative but one that is coherent and emotionally compelling.

With the advent of widespread adoption of social media, the opportunity for repeated exposure to misinformation has greatly increased. A study of 126,000 true and false news stories on Twitter, for example, found they were shared (retweeted) by 3 million people 4.5 million times.[167] False news stories spread more widely than true stories and did so more quickly. The tools that people use to access information have become a major contributor to peoples' acceptance of misinformation.

Cementing Misinformation: The Coherence of Knowledge

In discussing misinformation, the focus is often on a particular item of information – for example, a person's belief that ivermectin (an anti-parasitic agent) can cure Covid-19 (which multiple studies show it cannot do) – and on correcting the erroneous belief. As discussed in Section 2, that belief is embedded in a network of beliefs and buttressed by them. For example, hesitancy regarding Covid vaccination (a new item) is associated with related Covid beliefs such as the virus being manmade, that the vaccine was introduced too quickly to be safe, and pre-existing beliefs such as general vaccination hesitancy, belief in alternative medicine, and distrust of science, the pharmaceutical industry, and government.[168,169] This embedding suggests that addressing the one belief by itself rarely addresses the broader problem of the person's misinformation and that seeking to correct multiple linked misinformed beliefs will be more difficult.

Making the task even more difficult is the attraction of misinformation. Conspiracy theories provide a prime example. These are 'explanatory beliefs, involving multiple actors who join together in secret agreement and try to achieve a hidden goal that is perceived as unlawful or malevolent'.[170] Their attraction lies in peoples' need to make sense of their social environment, particularly when faced with uncontrollable (therefore threatening), complex, and distressing events, for example, a pandemic. Conspiracy theories provide a way to understand (make sense of) these events. Because it lends coherence, the fact that the theory could be not just wrong but even ludicrous or fanciful does not, for some people, make it less compelling, and their belief in the theory could be very strong. For those harbouring a strong distrust of government, the idea that Covid-19 was invented to allow for increased government control of the population and that Covid vaccines contain microchips that enable the government to track recipients is believable. Likewise, belief in other false claims such as 'natural' herbal concoctions billed as boosting the immune system to prevent Covid and 'alternative' remedies to cure it as substitutes for vaccination and medical intervention have been embraced. Of course, not everyone subscribes to conspiracy theories. Certain individual differences, for example, appear to be associated with belief in conspiracy theories, notably proneness to magical thinking, Machivellianism (seeking to manipulate others), selfishness, lack of caring, and a callous nature.[171]

Thus, the coherence of networked beliefs, their ability to address feelings of powerlessness, and perceptions of regaining control make misinformation attractive, reflecting a motivational component as well as a cognitive one. These are features that make misinformation believable and even attractive, thus more challenging to correct.[162,166]

Knowing You're Right: Commitment to Misinformation

A further difficulty is the confidence that people have about their knowledge. As discussed in Section 3, information search is often biased in favour of confirming current beliefs. In the context of the internet, the algorithms that respond to search queries and those determining content delivered on social media favour information that is consistent with prior viewing. This creates a cycle in which the searcher finds more and more information consistent with their current beliefs and grows more confident in those beliefs because of the constant presentation of consistent information. This has been called an echo chamber effect or reinforcing cycle in terms of media use.[140,172] This effect is exacerbated by overconfidence; people are often overly confident that they are informed and capable of making decisions and also feel they are typical so that their choice would be endorsed by relevant others.

Moreover, research on persuasion suggests that health consumers and patients can employ a range of strategies to maintain current beliefs, attitudes, and behaviours. These include information avoidance, counterargument, source derogation, biased processing strategies that reduce importance or isolate inconsistent information, and focus on consistent knowledge or social validation.[173] These efforts are triggered (motivated) by the person's perceptions of the persuasive attempts – notably when the attempts are seen as threats to personal autonomy (reactance), when they are not credible because they are inconsistent with prior beliefs and attitudes, or when they raise concerns of deception.

Corrective Campaigns

Despite the challenges posed by peoples' belief in and attachment to misinformation, there have been many attempts to correct the problem. In the US, the Lanham Act holds that firms can be liable for false or misleading advertising. Based on this law, the Federal Trade Commission (FTC) has sought various remedies for such advertising. Among these remedies, albeit rarely used, is mandated corrective advertising to address misleading marketing campaigns. The goal of the mandate is specifically to correct misleading or false claims in the advertising. For example, one company made the unsupported claim that its oil additive would decrease oil usage in a car. In response to an FTC complaint, a US government agency responsible for protecting consumers and promoting competition, the company agreed to place a corrective advertising statement in a number of periodicals, with the goal of correcting consumer misunderstanding of the product's benefits.[174] The success of corrective advertising campaigns has been measured with respect to short-term effects. In the case of the oil additive, there was no significant decrease in belief in advertising claims, although consumer purchase intentions decreased. However, long-term sales effects appeared to be negligible. In a related vein, banning cigarette advertising either partially or completely has no significant effect (by itself) on cigarette consumption.[175]

The limited success of corrective advertising campaigns reflects the challenge facing those seeking to correct the effects of misinformation. Addressing misinformation requires not only imparting knowledge but also correcting mistaken beliefs and research has shown that people who are misinformed can be very persistent in their beliefs.[176] Even if a person isn't motivated to resist the correction, he or she cannot simply forget the misinformation and substitute it with the correction. Retracting the information may at least temporarily tag the misinformation as false. If a correction is provided, it will be encoded as well, but often the misinformation enjoys greater familiarity through repetition so that after a time it regains its potency in deliberations as demonstrated in studies of the continued influence effect.[166] Moreover, unless the correction coheres with the rest of the person's beliefs, it will remain either suspect or somehow separate from the knowledge structure in which the misinformation fits. In either case, the removal of the misinformation creates a gap in the knowledge structure. In order to retain the coherence of the structure, the misinformation may be retained, particularly if the knowledge structure is consistent with a broader network of beliefs (frame of reference or worldview).[162,166]

Campaign Strategies

Guidelines for corrective campaigns have still been advanced. Messages can offer fact-based correction, attack logical fallacies in misinformation, and attack the credibility of the misinformation source.[162] The timing of the campaign can be prior to exposure to misinformation (prebunking) following the strategy of inoculation[177] or after exposure (debunking). Inoculation strategies can address likely misleading persuasive approaches people are likely to encounter. Debunking campaigns must address misinformation already in circulation. Repetition can be used against the misinformation by repeating the retraction.[166] Importantly, the effectiveness of retraction can be enhanced by providing an alternative account or narrative. Some success has been reported when the narrative addresses the motives of the source of misinformation. It has also been suggested that misinformation often offers a simple explanation and people prefer simple explanations. To the extent that the true explanation is more complex, nuanced, or bounded, it is important to emphasize the core of the argument and how it coheres with the larger information context. This may not be possible when the corrective information is inconsistent with the recipient's other beliefs and their worldview.

A vast literature has shown how difficult it can be to change strongly held attitudes. Corrective campaigns often enjoy limited success. The general limitations of mass media campaigns can be seen in studies of advertising. For example, a field experiment of advertising by the Anheuser-Busch company found that for a well-established brand, even eliminating advertising for a year in a group of markets had no effect on sales despite the continuation of competitor advertising.[178] Only after 18 months did sales begin to decline. Thus, 'a major objective of advertising ... may well be simply to reinforce and reiterate the fact that the brand exists, is eminently acceptable for use, and is widely available to consumers' (p. 233).[179]

Rather than attacking specific misinformation by providing corrections, broader goals have been proposed such as improved media, e-media, and news literacy, focusing particularly on the importance of scepticism and careful review of not only credentials but interests of information sources. Media literacy has been considered as a component of educational curricula and as a more focused intervention aimed at educating people on how to challenge media messages and protect themselves from their harmful effects.[180] However, the success of such interventions is mixed. For example, a study of social media self-disclosure found that media literacy had a constraining effect on intentions regarding self-disclosure but not on actual disclosure behaviours.[181]

Overall, then, misinformation is difficult to dislodge and the effectiveness of media and other mass audience campaigns is often limited. While there is evidence that deliberation decreases acceptance of misinformation, the problem remains that consumers and patients have limited expertise to discern the quality of medical information they encounter. This means that they must at some point decide who to trust to help them understand and evaluate the information and its implications for their health. This brings us back to the medical expert and the importance of the doctor–patient relationship.

5 The Doctor–Patient Relationship and Misinformation Management

To this point, misinformation has been portrayed as a problem arising from the interaction of the information environment and the way people think and feel about information they encounter. The amount of information presented to people has increased dramatically, but the quality of that information is decidedly mixed. At the same time, people's knowledge is fallible and given their biases in processing information, they can become misinformed. Compounding the problem is the difficulty of correcting misinformed beliefs. We would love to end, like a magician, by pulling a solution out of a hat, but unfortunately such a solution would be, like the magic trick, an illusion. What has become clear through previous sections is that correcting misinformation involves much more than corrective content. Simply telling people they are wrong and providing the 'truth' is unlikely to be successful. Misinformation is often seductive – it may offer certainty if not comfort. Covid-19 isn't really such a big problem, and if you get it, it's not your fault, even if you attended a big birthday party last week without a mask. Blame the government, the experts, the pharmaceutical companies. Still, we should not throw up our hands in despair. Some efforts succeed, and they suggest possible approaches.

This section focuses on the important role that trust might play in counteracting misinformation, notably trust within a doctor–patient relationship that could privilege the physician in preventing patients from becoming misinformed, countering misinformation already held by patients, and improving patient understanding of their health problems and concerns. Mutual trust is a central requirement for efficacious relationships between doctor and patient, and the trust patients' place in their doctors is the major currency of the relationship. Trust grounds a collaborative doctor–patient relationship (therapeutic alliance) which in turn plays a critical role in promoting accurate patient knowledge, understanding, and healthy choices. Moreover, a trusting doctor–patient relationship frees the patient from a dangerous 'going it alone' vision of autonomy. It allows the patient 'to exercise their autonomy by relinquishing some decision-making power to those with the expertise to care for them. Physicians then act as entrusted fiduciaries' (p. 18).[24]

Dead Ends

The importance of a strong, trusting doctor–patient relationship can be seen in some unproductive alternatives. Mentioned earlier were new regulations making medical records available to patients, seeking to enable them to take greater control of their health decisions. However, giving patients access to technical data like diagnostic scans and the radiologist's notes is unlikely to advance this goal. The scan itself requires specialized expertise to read and interpret. The radiologist's notes are likely to be cryptic for the patient because of the technical terminology and the assumed knowledge of the expected recipient – the patient's physician. It is that physician's specialized knowledge and experience that enables the physician to understand not only the specific information provided by the scan but also to situate that information in a larger corpus of knowledge about the patient and his or her health condition. Only then does the information have diagnostic and prognostic value. For the patient, by contrast, the likely outcome may be more but certainly not better information. Reading the notes may be frustrating and anxiety-provoking. Rather than being better informed, providing the information without guidance offers an illusion of transparency.

Another doomed approach focuses on restricting health information on the internet. Advocates of a more truthful internet in the realm of health face severe challenges, regardless of whether gaps in knowledge are to be closed, erroneous information avoided or corrected, or misinformation needs to be removed. If one were to seek to ban health misinformation from the internet, what exactly would be banned and what would be added to close knowledge gaps? What about information and advice that is accurate and helpful for some people but inapplicable or even dangerous for others? In short, any such attempt would create tremendous definition problems, legal issues in civil rights, and would require a level of goodwill in international cooperation that is unimaginable. Given these hindrances, it is no wonder that efforts in this direction have failed.[182,183]

These dead ends highlight two givens regarding health information. First, giving people more of it doesn't make them more enlightened or less likely to access misinformation. Second, patient access to new media information cannot be restricted. Information they can't understand or interpret is readily available, along with information that is not relevant to them. Moreover, a cornucopia of misinformation will present itself. Some of it gains credibility coming from social media contacts and new artificial intelligence tools produce materials that seem authoritative even if they are entirely fictitious. For example, one such tool generated a legal brief that was submitted to a court and was accepted until it was found that six of the case precedents cited were fabricated by the artificial intelligence tool itself.[184]

If access to information, good and bad, is bound to increase, the central task will be to guide people as consumers and patients to attend to information that is accurate and relevant to them. One opportunity lies in using the professional's specialized knowledge to help patients understand how to make sense of the information they access and why the misinformation is wrong and how it could hurt them. As we argued in Section 4, countering mistaken beliefs must be more than correction, and even well-designed communication campaigns fail. This leaves a central role for the physician.[185] To explore this possibility, we consider three crucial elements of the patient-doctor relationship: (1) the nature and role of trust, (2) the challenges of new communication technologies, and (3) the tasks and opportunities for addressing misinformation.

Trust in an Evolving Social Environment

As discussed in Section 1, the ethical practice of medicine invokes four norms: (1) respect for autonomy, (2) nonmaleficence, (3) beneficence), and (4) justice.[23] To say that a patient trusts a physician means the patient believes the physician is acting in accordance with these norms. In particular, the patient must believe that, while respecting their autonomy, the physician seeks to relieve, lessen, or prevent harm and provide benefits, balancing them against risks and costs. In short, the patient must believe that the physician is acting for their benefit. To a significant extent, medical care is what economists call a credence good. That is, the quality of the doctor's care is not observable. The patient consults the doctor and the doctor prescribes a medication, performs a procedure, or even suggests that the patient just get rest and drink fluids. The patient recovers, but is this due to whatever the doctor did? Even if so, could the doctor have done something different that would have speeded recovery, reduced discomfort, or lowered risk? Trust means that the patient believes the doctor 'did the right thing'. The social environment surrounding medical care presents significant challenges to this trust.

Challenges of Modern Healthcare to Patient Trust

The profound changes to the healthcare delivery system since the 1950s present challenges to patient trust. One important challenge arises from the depersonalization of the doctor–patient relationship. The doctor–patient dyad has long been a guiding principle of medicine.[186,187] Within this personal relationship, sometimes compared with friendship, the doctor and patient meet each other without external influences. The duty of confidentiality imposed on the doctor contributes to the preservation of this relationship, as does the fact that the medical professional can expect the patient to place his or her full trust in him or her. Because of this relationship of trust, communication between doctor and patient can flourish despite the knowledge asymmetry between doctor and patient. In recent years, this pattern of personal relationship has been increasingly challenged by the institutional arrangements of healthcare. First, the growth of medical knowledge has led to greater reliance on specialists. Specialized medical knowledge is a hallmark of the progress of medicine since the 1950s, providing incalculable benefits to patients. There is, however, a price to pay. With the increasing level of specialization in medicine, the patient must interact not only with his or her GP but with several specialized physicians. An urban US cancer patient will be referred by the GP to a cancer centre, where the patient will be seen by an oncologist as well as other specialists such as a radiation oncologist, surgeon, nurses who administer many kinds of treatment, a palliative care physician for quality-of-life concerns including pain management, and allied health professionals including dieticians and physical therapists. This panoply of specialized care may shift the bases for trust. As in the past, if the patient sees a physician on a repeated basis (e.g., the GP or oncologist), the continuity provides a basis for the development of a personal relationship in which trust is based on each knowing the other's likely behaviour in their interactions as well as mutual respect. With the other specialists, trust in technical expertise is the paramount concern as evidenced by credentials and reputation.[188] Patients still want relationships with specialists, but they focus on being treated as an individual and being respected – a member of the care team with legitimate opinions.

Coincident with the growth of specialization, the doctor and patient have been placed increasingly in a corporate structure of healthcare provision with the development of managed care, in which a corporate entity like a Health

Maintenance Organization (HMO) or insurance company takes a role in structuring the interface between doctor and patient.[22] In the case of insurance companies, the interface highlights economic aspects of access to and quality of care. The HMO places limits on consumer choice of providers. These changes led to 'anonymization'[189] or 'depersonalization'[190] of the patient's relationship with the healthcare system, embedding that with the physician. This shift has raised concerns about trust by highlighting a transactional view of medical care constrained by limited choice either within the service network of the HMO or the payment limits imposed by insurance. This is not to say that trust has been lost entirely. In a 2014 study, only 23% of Americans reported high confidence in the healthcare system and 58% reported that physicians could be trusted, much lower than in many other countries,[191] for example, Switzerland (83%), UK (76%), and France (75%). However, 56% of Americans reported high levels of satisfaction with the treatment they received when they last visited a doctor, higher than that reported in the UK (51%) and France (38%). Americans hate the system but seem satisfied with their doctors' care. In most managed care systems, the patient has a primary physician – a GP in the British system or a primary care physician in the US. The maintenance of a trusting doctor–patient relationship is conceptually important to these corporate entities, who recognize its importance to patient participation, compliance, and health outcomes. Nevertheless, building and maintaining that trusting relationship is more challenging than in earlier times. For example, continuity by itself does not guarantee trust. In these new healthcare arrangements, it is possible for a patient to experience continuity with a physician for whom they feel low trust, in which case, unsurprisingly, continuity doesn't contribute to patient satisfaction.[192] Trust is conditioned on the patient's perception that the physician is working for their benefit – providing needed information and evidence-based *personalized* recommendations.[193]

Challenges of the Internet to Patient Trust

The internet has become a central place for patients seeking health-related information, which has also impacted the doctor–patient relationship. For most patients, this impact is not direct. After searching health information on the internet, patients report greater confidence in discussing their health with physicians, more confidence in the physician's advice, and more empowerment to participate in managing their health.[185] Most patients feel that bringing information from the internet to their consultation with a physician either doesn't affect their relationship with their physician or improves it. Patients report their trust in their doctor; they attest to the quality and strength of that trust, and they emphasize the necessity of having their doctor to consult.[194] Patients desire their physicians' expertise to help them understand and interpret internet information, particularly its accuracy as well as its relevance to their condition. Even with patients' concern for autonomy and independence,[195,196] information-seeking on the internet is often aimed at the background of a disease rather than replacing the consultation about it with the physician. In other words, patients recognize the critical importance of the physician, especially his or her ability to tailor the responses and advice provided to the patient's specific medical condition, their expressed concerns, and their ability and readiness to cope with the information. Delivering on these expectations can be challenging in the current healthcare setting.

New Communication Technologies and the Challenge of Misinformation

The growth of misinformation broadcast through the internet and social media was discussed in Section 1, and as noted above, efforts to prevent patients from accessing it are doomed to failure. It is important to recognize and accept new communication technologies as part of the background of the times and mores that affect all of us, including healthcare providers and patients.[185,197] It is also important to recognize that people are grappling with change of an extraordinary scope and pace. The internet and the many tools made available through it have dramatically changed the information environment healthcare consumers face when making decisions about their health.[198] On the upside, this includes but extends well beyond offering health information. A range of offerings are available to help consumers gather information about their health and health problems and navigate the healthcare system. Examples include:

- knowledge compilation as a service by healthcare institutions, such as the Mayo Clinic
- compilation for easy access to media coverage of health topics
- decision aids, for example, criteria for deciding whether to seek testing for BRCA (BReast CAncer) genetic cancer markers
- patient-oriented diagnostic tools
- doctor and hospital portals that make the organization of treatment easier
- physician and hospital ratings
- shared patient experiences and emotional support

The downside, of course, is the amount of material posted on the internet and promulgated through social media that is less constructive or misinformed.[199] Some, like advertising, are not explicitly incorrect but may be problematic in their emphases, as in the case of DTCA. Some internet information may be confusing because conflicting findings lead to differing medical interpretations and recommendations. Other material is explicitly misinformed. Some may be based on outdated studies that have been superseded by newer data or inappropriately applied findings. Some employ pseudoscience or 'junk' science, as in the case of vaccination and autism. Some create commercial differentiation that provides no functional advantage.[200] Finally, some is completely fabricated – for example, that an extract of apricot pits can cure cancer. And no effective means to make it easier for consumers to identify such misinformation as problematic has been found.[201–204] Moreover, as discussed in Sections 3 and 4, people exhibit biases in their approach to information, overconfidence in their grasp of information, and persistence in their beliefs that make correcting mistaken beliefs difficult.

The information resources offered by the internet thus complicate the physician's task. With the internet, the physician can no longer prevent the intrusion of false or irrelevant information. Anybody can post their views on health matters, no matter how unqualified or inexperienced and whatever their motives. The information consumers can retrieve from the internet can be correct or incorrect, relevant or irrelevant.[205–208] Health information and misinformation is searched, found, looked at, and used in various ways by consumers,[91,92,134] often prior to consultation with a doctor, but postconsultation information-seeking also occurs.[209] At the same time, knowledge gained from health information on the internet, even when accurate and relevant, does not necessarily make health decisions easier for patients. At least for some patients, the availability of information increased knowledge but also increased insecurity, and the higher involvement associated with increased knowledge meant greater felt responsibility. As might be expected, not all patients find this responsibility appealing[210,211] so the physician must be sensitive to the patient's desired role in decision-making.

Processing, understanding, and remembering internet information places severe demands on consumers' health literacy. When consumers confront their healthcare providers with the information they hold, the wealth of health information available through the internet becomes a challenge to the healthcare provider too. Beyond the traditional task of providing the patient with the information necessary for his or her treatment, physicians must increasingly address information and misinformation patients bring to the consultation. As information provision has become more important in line with today's ideals for patients to be actively involved in medical decisions,[14,212–215] physicians may find themselves in the role of their patients' information manager.[92,216] Once again, the trust a patient accords to his or her doctor is essential in making this possible. Physicians cannot prevent patients from accessing misinformation, but they are in a privileged position to help patients capitalize on the wealth of valid and relevant information available and understand why the misinformation patients uncover should be ignored.

Unfortunately, research on how physicians can or should undertake the task of correcting misinformation is very limited. Some perspectives based on clinical experience and cases have been advanced:

- Offer assistance in decision-making rather than attacking information sources or trying to persuade.[217]
- Be sensitive to the patient's background and experiences (medical errors, historic inequities, religious beliefs).
- Educate patients about evaluating information and sources, inviting questions, engaging patients in understanding the evolving science relating to their health problems, sharing trustworthy sources.[199]

All of these perspectives, it is noted, are built on the physician's relationship with the patient. Listening to the patient and tailoring responses to their specific knowledge failures and information needs, that is, meeting the patient where he or she is, and building patient trust.

Physicians Confronting Patient Misinformation

In any interaction between a patient and a physician, misunderstandings are common and can grow out of one or more mechanisms:

1. The patient is pursuing the wrong goal by turning to the doctor.
2. The patient's goal is appropriate, but he doesn't know what information is relevant for reaching it and, therefore, cannot distinguish between relevant and irrelevant information.
3. The patient understands the relevance of the information but misunderstands its meaning in the context of his own health problem.

Certainly, such mechanisms plagued patients and physicians before the advent of the internet. Physicians have always had to correct patients' faulty expectations, guide patients to relevant information, and correct mistakes in the patient's knowledge. Contemporary digital communication gives the patient easy access to types of information he or she is not familiar with and will often have trouble understanding, magnifying the patient's potential misunderstanding. A doctor, in contrast, will be familiar with much medical information and can now get it much more easily. This widening asymmetry means that the physician's information management tasks are magnified as well.

For the physician, insufficient health literacy in a patient presents a complex problem. From the professional's viewpoint, the health decision pertaining to the patient should focus on information that is correct and important for the decision and ignore everything that is false or irrelevant. When doctor and patient agree on the information and its meaning for the patient's health situation, they are likely to agree on the actions to take, so it is of no import who will make the decision.[218] However, the patient's perspective on what information is true and relevant may differ from the professional's, creating consultation scenarios shown in the conceptual model in Figure 3. The scenarios present a variety of challenges to the professional, who is placed in the position of negotiating information relevance in order to guide the patient's judgements. Even if the professional wants the consumer to be engaged and empowered in reaching a decision,[219,220] it is critical from the professional's perspective that the patient's judgements and decisions are based on a solid grounding of relevant and valid information. Otherwise, the physician faces some unpalatable options – preventing or limiting the patient's influence on the decision, terminating the treatment relationship, or accepting the patient's mistaken choice.

Professional training provides the physician with the expertise to distinguish information that is important and useful for the patient from that which is dangerous, misleading, or irrelevant. The patient, lacking this expertise, is likely to view information from a personal perspective – as information the patient feels she needs and wants, information about which she doesn't care, and that she doesn't want. The critical problem is that, because of these differing perspectives, neither health literacy nor empowerment will prevent the doctor and patient's perception of information from diverging.[231] The problem is characterized in Figure 3. The 'Consistent' cells are those where the doctor and patient agree that the information is true and important to health decisions or agree that the information is false and dangerous so should not be applied to health decisions. From the professional perspective, focusing on important information is crucial as is ignoring dangerous or misleading information and the importance of these agreements must be reinforced. The critical problems arise in the 'Inconsistent' cells. One problem comes from information that is dangerous or misleading that the patient through an illusionary literacy believes is valid and important. The physician's communication task is to convince the patient that such information is either dangerous or at least irrelevant. The converse is important information the patient perceives as unimportant or because of preconceived notions or fear finds threatening. Here the task of the doctor becomes one of education and persuasion to convince the patient of the value of considering the information. A similar but perhaps less onerous task is

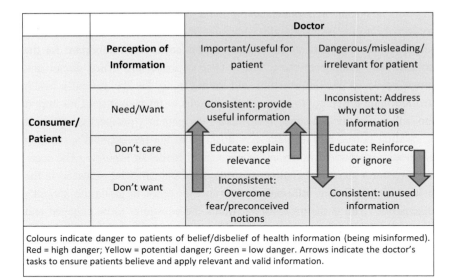

		Doctor	
	Perception of Information	Important/useful for patient	Dangerous/misleading/ irrelevant for patient
Consumer/ Patient	Need/Want	Consistent: provide useful information	Inconsistent: Address why not to use information
	Don't care	Educate: explain relevance	Educate: Reinforce or ignore
	Don't want	Inconsistent: Overcome fear/preconceived notions	Consistent: unused information

Colours indicate danger to patients of belief/disbelief of health information (being misinformed). Red = high danger; Yellow = potential danger; Green = low danger. Arrows indicate the doctor's tasks to ensure patients believe and apply relevant and valid information.

Figure 3 Doctor–patient information alignment.

presented by the 'Educate' cells where the patient doesn't care about the information so the physician must either stress the importance of relevant information or warn against or simply ignore misinformation. In the context of a patient visit, the doctor may face several pieces of information falling into different cells. This requires the physician to be adaptive – 'meeting patients where they are'.

The persuasive character of some contemporary medical consultations brings these conversations under the rubric of strategic communication. Physicians must think beforehand how they will be able to address the misinformed patient without giving away too much ground, but also trying to avoid hurting their opponent – their patient. The existence of strategic thinking before consultation with a patient was demonstrated in a study that interviewed, in a semi-structured design, 17 physicians living in the Italian-speaking part of Switzerland. The physicians related a number of considerations they think through when preparing for consultations that are likely to turn into a strategic mode. These considerations can be summarized into four classes: resistance to online information, repairing online information, co-construction around online information, and enhancement of online information.

The model in Figure 3 identifies the doctor's communication tasks but does not explain how they are to be accomplished. Doctor–patient interaction and relationship have traditionally served as the basis for preventing misunderstandings. Prior to the advent of broadened information availability, the doctor served as an information gatekeeper. In the changed healthcare environment with dramatically increased information availability and expanded expectations of patient involvement in decisions, how can misinformation be minimized and managed?

In an unpublished study, Lu and Schulz first asked physicians about their perceptions of patients' internet information-seeking behaviour and whether any antecedents (patient characteristics) would predict certain perceptions. Then, physicians were asked about their communication strategies and their difficulties dealing with internet-informed patients (IIP). Two broad groups of physicians were identified. One group considered the internet a legitimate information tool and showed generally positive perceptions of patients' online information searches. The other group had stronger feelings of threatened authority and distrust from IIP. Corresponding to their general perceptions, some physicians adopted a participative strategy to collaborate with IIP and guide them to interpret internet information. The others took the defensive approach to block or discourage patients from online searches. Physicians' judgement of a specific patient and communication context will affect their attitude and the adoption of communicative strategies.

Given the information environment and the centrality of the internet for patients, it is doubtful that seeking to dissuade them from using the internet as an information resource will be successful as a strategy for addressing misinformation. Collaborating seems the more promising approach. The physician can build on patient trust to persuade patients of what is important and what should be ignored. For those who are largely uninformed, this strategy would be reasonable. However, for patients whose misinformation is embedded in a background network of related beliefs, many of which are likewise false or else irrelevant to the particular health problem or decision, correcting the misinformation and all of this background is unlikely to be successful even if the physician were to take the time to try. An alternative might be to position the accurate information and a network of related information (a coherent story) as exceptional – something specific to the patient or their health condition to be shared by the doctor and patient. This change of frame would place the story and the decision outside the misinformed background. Trust here is central – the credibility of the story depends on it and forms the basis for the physician's ability to grapple with misinformation more effectively than impersonal corrective campaigns.

The essence of the professional, in a traditional sense, as we have seen, is trustworthiness in both expertise and beneficence. In earlier times, one could depend on the professional – doctor, lawyer, or accountant. He or she held information that was imperfectly understood (if even available) to the layman. In many cases, the information would be literally unintelligible (e.g., employing Latin terms). As important, the expectation was that the professional would work for the benefit of the client or patient, and despite increased recognition of the patient's autonomy, beneficence remains central to the physician's treatment of the patient. The physician remains committed to the well-being of the patient, and the patient's trust is central to the physician's ability to achieve that end. This requires that the professional build a trusting relationship, but such a relationship entails expectations on both sides. The professional has to provide, through language and action, evidence of adherence to ethical values, including recognition of patient autonomy. On the other side, the patient has a stronger voice but also must assume some responsibility in managing their health. This, as noted earlier, leads to a constrained collaboration. A strong doctor–patient relationship can address this constraint by advancing beyond a transactional vision of doctor/patient interaction (advice for payment) to one of more generalized exchanges, where the general welfare of the doctor/patient pair is considered.[24] In short, the basis of relationships is changing but the task of conveying knowledge remains, and the importance of the professional relationship is enhanced.

Certainly, the doctor's office and the formal interaction in the consultation lend weight to the physician's statements and recommendations. However, trust and credibility are not confined to the doctor's office. The same approach of evidencing caring (beneficence) and respect (autonomy) can be effective even in casual social settings. An anecdote related to the authors demonstrates this. A physician at a swimming pool was chatting with a fellow swimmer she just met. The woman was planning an international trip but had not been vaccinated for Covid-19. The physician asked the woman about her concerns, which focused on the speed with which the vaccines were developed and their attendant risks, a common comment at the time promoted by anti-vaccination groups. The physician explained the extensive history of related research that long preceded the pandemic, the extensive multi-stage testing for safety and efficacy conducted on the vaccine, the physician's own experience getting vaccinated, and her harrowing experiences caring for Covid patients. When they met again a few weeks later, the woman had received a vaccination. The approach – one-on-one, person-centred, caring and respectful – a conversation between strangers where there was no issue of gain for the physician but capitalizing on her credentialed expertise, was effective in overcoming misinformation.

Taking a Long View

Misinformation has garnered headlines and has had undeniably negative effects on people's health. It is estimated, for example, that by May 2022, 319,000 unvaccinated people in the US died from Covid-19 after vaccines were available. A large proportion of these deaths were due to misinformation about the safety and efficacy of Covid-19 vaccines. Those spreading such misinformation have much to answer for. Still, in the US, trust in health agencies like the US Centers for Disease Control and medical leaders remains robust, and more than 68% of people received a full initial course of Covid-19 vaccinations, a rate that exceeds 75% in most Western European countries.[221,222] Not everyone becomes misinformed.

Another case suggests that over a longer term, progress is possible. Consider cigarette smoking in the US – a scourge implicated in 480,000 deaths each year.[232] Cigarette smoking was popular in the US by the early twentieth century and, supported by a great deal of advertising, consumption grew from 54 cigarettes per adult in 1900 to a peak of 4,345 in 1963. Prior to 1964, most people were misinformed about the dangers of smoking. Indeed, during World War I, cigarette smoking was supported by physicians to ease pain for wounded soldiers. It wasn't until 1964 that the Surgeon General's report was published linking smoking to lung cancer and other respiratory diseases. Cigarette manufacturers denied the link even though they agreed to stop advertising on radio and television in 1969. By 1990, smoking was banned on all commercial airline flights in the US, followed by a ban on most European airline flights in 1999. Smoking bans in public places have greatly expanded, and in 1999, outdoor advertising was discontinued. Taxation has proved to be a major factor in reducing cigarette sales; in the US taxes account on average for 42% of the retail cost and in the UK 82%. Globally, efforts to decrease smoking have been launched building on World Health Organization recommendations and their effects tallied. Activities that may play a role include anti-smoking media campaigns, package warning labels, banning advertising and promotion, smoke-free policies for public spaces, increased availability and affordability of cessation programs, and taxation of cigarette sales. Physicians played an important role in reducing smoking. Beyond counselling patients, by the 1980s, physician-delivered smoking cessation programs were being tested and implemented. Medical support tools were developed and promoted by physicians including nicotine replacement (first as a prescription drug in the 1980s and later OTC) and more recently varenicline in 2006. The effectiveness of these physician interventions have been demonstrated in numerous studies.[223–226] All of these efforts have had a major impact. Since 1964, the prevalence of cigarette smoking in the US has fallen from 42.4% in 1965 to 17.8% in 2013. Yet, even today, misinformation about smoking safety persists. In a 2010 study of smokers in France, 38% believed smoking causes cancer only for those who smoke more than they did.[227] Thus, over a period of fifty years, the combination of health campaigns and medical interventions have enjoyed substantial success.

Taking a longer view of misinformation on the internet, as our experience with the internet increases, people are growing more savvy about what they encounter. A 2018 study by the Pew Research Center found that adults aged 18–49 were better than those 50 and older at distinguishing between statements of fact and opinion in the news and this was independent of liberal versus conservative appeal of the statements.[228] Perhaps the catalogue of disappointment that introduced this monograph can be overcome.

Conclusion

The growth of patient empowerment as a right and as a responsibility has increased the involvement of consumers in managing their health and patients in making medical decisions. Along with this change, the explosion of health information available today, particularly online, has profoundly altered the consumer information environment. Unfortunately, the internet and social media have also made available a great deal of misinformation, and the way people approach and process information places them at risk of accepting that misinformation as true. What makes misinformation insidious for people is that the same processes that allow people to become knowledgeable about a topic can also make them prone to become misinformed. Because of the persistence of beliefs in misinformation, it has created problems, in some cases crises, for people's health. Countering misinformation is challenging, and the case of cigarette smoking suggests that there is no single tool that will solve the problem. Coordinated campaigns, public policy, and interventions at the individual level by medical experts, particularly physicians, together offer a plausible route to success. Again taking a long view, education to make people more literate about health but also sceptical and deliberate in their acceptance and use of health information, will be central to helping people be more successful as empowered health consumers.

References

1. World Health Organization. *Definition of Health*, vol. 2011. apps.who.int/aboutwho/en/definition.html (2011).
2. van Dulmen, S., Sluijs, E., van Dijk, L., et al. Patient adherence to medical treatment: A review of reviews. *BMC Health Serv Res* **7**, 55 (2007).
3. European Centre for Disease Prevention and Control. *COVID-19 Vaccine Tracker*. (October 2023). https://vaccinetracker.ecdc.europa.eu/public/extensions/covid-19/vaccine-tracker.html#uptake-tab.
4. World Health Organization. *Adherence to Long-term Therapies: Evidence for Action*. (World Health Organization, 2003).
5. Jones, L., Sciamanna, C. & Lehman, E. Are those who use specific complementary and alternative medicine therapies less likely to be immunized? *Prev Med* **50**, 148–154 (2010).
6. Ball, P. & Maxmen, A. The epic battle against coronavirus misinformation and conspiracy theories. *Nature* **581**, 371–374 (2020).
7. Kuklinski, J. H., Quirk, P. J., Jerit, J., Schwieder, D. & Rich, R. F. Misinformation and the currency of democratic citizenship. *J Polit* **62**, 790–816 (2000).
8. Hameleers, M., Brosius, A., de Vreese, C. H., et al. Mistake or manipulation? Conceptualizing perceived mis- and disinformation among news consumers in 10 European countries. *Commun Res* **49**, 919–941 doi:10.1177/0093650221997719 (2022).
9. Walter, N. & Tukachinsky, R. A meta-analytic examination of the continued influence of misinformation in the face of correction: How powerful is it, Why does it happen, and how to stop it? *Commun Res* **47**, 155–177 (2020).
10. Wang, Y., McKee, M., Torbica, A. & Stuckler, D. Systematic literature review on the spread of health-related misinformation on social media. *Soc Sci Med* **240**, 112552. Preprint at https://doi.org/10.1016/j.socscimed.2019.112552 (2019).
11. Dunning, D. The Dunning–Kruger effect. On being ignorant of one's own ignorance. *Adv Exp Soc Psychol* **44**, 247–296 (2011).
12. Andrus, M. R. & Roth, M. T. Health literacy: A review. *Pharmacotherapy* **22**, 282–302 (2002).
13. Rubinelli, S., Schulz, P. J. & Nakamoto, K. Health literacy beyond knowledge and behaviour: Letting the patient be a patient. *Int J Public Health* **54**, 307–311 (2009).

14. Funnell, M. M., Anderson, R. M., Arnold, M. S., et al. Empowerment: An idea whose time has come in diabetes education. *Diabetes Educ* **17**, 37–41 (1991).
15. Schulz, P. J. & Nakamoto, K. Health literacy and patient empowerment in health communication: The importance of separating conjoined twins. *Patient Educ Couns* **90**, 4–11 (2013).
16. Osler, W. *The Evolution of Modern Medicine*. (Yale University Press, 1921).
17. Thomas, D. P. The demise of bloodletting. *J R Coll Physicians Edinb* **44**, 72–77 (2014).
18. Shorter, E. *Doctors and Their Patients: A Social History*. (Taylor and Francis, 1991).
19. Crellin, J. K. Folklore and medicines – medical interfaces: A kaleidoscope and challenge. *Pharm Hist* **55**, 104–111 (2013).
20. Merten, J. W., Gordon, B. T., King, J. L. & Pappas, C. Cannabidiol (CBD): Perspectives from Pinterest. *Subst Use Misuse* **55**, 2213–2220 (2020).
21. Boyaji, S., Merkow, J., Elman, R. N. M., et al. The role of cannabidiol (CBD) in chronic pain management: An assessment of current evidence. *Curr Pain Headache Rep* **24**, 1–6 (2020).
22. Starr, P. *The Social Transformation of American Medicine*. (Basic Books, Inc., 1982).
23. Beauchamp, T. L. & Childress, J. F. *Principles of biomedical ethics*. (Oxford University Press, 2013).
24. Tauber, A. *Patient Autonomy and the Ethics of Responsibility*. (The MIT Press, 2005).
25. Hippocrates. The Oath. In *Ancient Medicine. Airs, Waters, Places. Epidemics 1 and 3. The Oath. Precepts. Nutriment* (ed. Jones, W. H. S. (transl.)) 298–299 (Harvard University Press, 1923).
26. Faden, R. R. & Beauchamp, T. L. *A History and Theory of Informed Consent*. (Oxford University Press, 1986).
27. Katz, J. *The Silent World of Doctor and Patient*. (Johns Hopkins University Press, 2002).
28. Irving, G., Neves, A. L., Dambha-Miller, H., et al. International variations in primary care physician consultation time: A systematic review of 67 countries. *BMJ Open* **7**, e017902 (2017).
29. World Health Organization. *Health Promotion*. www.who.int/teams/health-promotion/enhanced-wellbeing/first-global-conference.
30. Bhopal, R. S. & White, M. Health promotion for ethnic minorities: Past, present and future. In *'Race' and Health in Contemporary Britain* (ed. Ahmad, W. I. U.) 137–166 (Open University Press, 1993).

31. Rissel, C. Empowerment: The holy grail of health promotion? *Health Promot Int* **9**, 39–47 (1994).

32. Neuhauser, D. The coming third health care revolution: Personal empowerment. *Qual Manag Health Care* **12**, 171–176 (2003).

33. Edwards, M., Davies, M. & Edwards, A. What are the external influences on information exchange and shared decision-making in healthcare consultations: A meta-synthesis of the literature. *Patient Educ Couns* **75**, 37–52 (2009).

34. Salmon, P., George, D., Hall, M. & Frca, D. Patient empowerment or the emperor's new clothes. *J R Soc Med* **97**, 53–56 (2004).

35. Levinson, W., Kao, A., Kuby, A. & Thisted, R. A. Not all patients want to participate in decision making: A national study of public preferences. *J Gen Intern Med* **20**, 531–535 (2005).

36. Manson, N. C. Why do patients want information if not to take part in decision making? *J Med Ethics* **36**, 834–837 (2010).

37. Vinson, A. H. 'Constrained collaboration': Patient empowerment discourse as resource for countervailing power. *Sociol Health Illn* **38**, 1364–1378 (2016).

38. Pilnick, A. & Dingwall, R. On the remarkable persistence of asymmetry in doctor/patient interaction: A critical review. *Soc Sci Med* **72**, 1374–1382 (2011).

39. Zarcadoolas, C., Pleasant, A. & Greer, D. S. *Advancing health literacy: A framework for understanding and action.* (Wiley, 2006).

40. DeBuono, B. Health literacy: A hidden and critical challenge to effective health care. *AHIP Cover* **45**, 38–40 (2004).

41. Dewalt, D. A., Berkman, N. D., Sheridan, S., Lohr, K. N. & Pignone, M. P. Literacy and health outcomes: A systematic review of the literature. *J Gen Intern Med* **19**, 1228–1239 (2004).

42. Mancuso, C. A. & Rincon, M. Impact of health literacy on longitudinal asthma outcomes. *J Gen Intern Med* **21**, 813–817 (2006).

43. Schillinger, D., Grumbach, K., Piette, J., et al. Association of health literacy with diabetes outcomes. *JAMA* **288**, 475–482 (2002).

44. Wolf, M. S., Gazmararian, J. A. & Baker, D. W. Health literacy and functional health status among older adults. *Arch Intern Med* **165**, 1946–1952 (2005).

45. Brown, S. A. Studies of educational interventions and outcomes in diabetic adults: A meta-analysis revisited. *Patient Educ Couns* **16**, 189–215 (1990).

46. Lavelle-Jones, C., Byrne, D. J., Rice, P. & Cuschieri, A. Factors affecting quality of informed consent. *Br Med J* **306**, 885–890 (1993).

47. Cassileth, B. R., Zupkis, R. V., Sutton-Smith, K. & March, V. Informed consent – Why are its goals imperfectly realized? *N Engl J Med* **302**, 896–900 (1980).

48. Keller, K. L. & Staelin, R. Effects of quality and quantity of information on decision effectiveness. *J Consumer Res* **14**, 200 (1987).

49. Velo, G. & Moretti, U. Direct-to-consumer information in Europe: The blurred margin between promotion and information. *Br J Clin Pharmacol* **66**, 626–628 (2008).

50. Between, D. Direct-to-consumer advertising under fire. *Bull World Health Organ* **87**, 576–577. Preprint at https://doi.org/10.2471/BLT.09.040809 (2009).

51. Ventola, C. L. Direct-to-consumer pharmaceutical advertising therapeutic or toxic? *P and T* **36**, 669–684 (2011).

52. Thaul, S. *Direct to Consumer Advertising of Prescription Drugs.* Congressional Research Service. http://assets.opencrs.com/rpts/R40590_20090520.pdf.

53. Liang, B. A. & Mackey, T. Direct-to-consumer advertising with interactive internet media: Global regulation and public health issues. *JAMA* **305**, 824–825 (2011).

54. Marks, J. The price of seduction: Direct-to-consumer advertising of prescription drugs in the US. *N C Med J* **64**, 292–295 (2003).

55. U.S. Food and Drug Administration. *The Impact of Direct-to-Consumer Advertising* (2013).

56. Mintzes, B. Advertising of prescription-only medicines to the public: Does evidence of benefit counterbalance harm? *Annu Rev Public Health* **33**, 259–277 (2012).

57. Frosch, D. L., Grande, D., Tarn, D. M. & Kravitz, R. L. A decade of controversy: Balancing policy with evidence in the regulation of prescription drug advertising. *Am J Public Health* **100**, 24–32 (2010).

58. Delbaere, M. & Smith, M. C. Health care knowledge and consumer learning: The case of direct-to-consumer drug advertising. *Health Mark Q* **23**, 9–29 (2006).

59. Aikin, K. (FDA). *Patient and Physician Attitudes and Behaviors Associated with DTC Promotion of Prescription Drugs – Summary of FDA Survey Research Results. Notes* (2004).

60. Donohue, J. M., Cevasco, M. & Rosenthal, M. B. A decade of direct-to-consumer advertising of prescription drugs. *N Engl J Med* **357**, 673–681 (2007).

61. Almasi, E. a. , Stafford, R. S., Kravitz, R. L. & Mansfield, P. R. What are the public health effects of direct-to-consumer drug advertising? *PLoS Med* **3**, 284–288 (2006).

62. Davis J. The effect of qualifying language on perceptions of drug appeal, drug experience, and estimates of side-effect incidence in DTC advertising. *J Health Commun* **12**, 607–622 (2007).

63. Frosch, D. L., Krueger, P. M., Hornik, R. C. & Barg, F. K. Creating demand for prescription drugs: A content analysis of television direct-to-consumer advertising – Table 2. Proportion of advertisements that present factual claims, appeals, lifestyle, and medication themes. *Ann Fam Med* **5**, 6–13 (2007).

64. Conrad P. *The Medicalization of Society: On the Transformation of Human Conditions into Treatable Disorders*. (The Johns Hopkins University Press, 2007).

65. Moynihan, R., Heath, I. & Henry, D. Selling sickness: The pharmaceutical industry and disease mongering. *BMJ* **324**, 886–891 (2002).

66. *Most Popular Email Providers in History – Statistics and Data*. Last Accessed: 3 February 2024. https://statisticsanddata.org/data/most-popular-email-providers-in-history/.

67. CERN. *A Short History of the Web*. CERN. Last Accessed: 3 February 2024. https://home.cern/science/computing/birth-web/short-history-web.

68. Coffman, K. & Odlysco, A. M. The size and growth rate of the internet. *First Monday* **3**(10), (1998).

69. *Internet Growth Statistics 1995 to 2022 – The Global Village Online*. Last Accessed: 3 February 2024. www.internetworldstats.com/emarketing.htm.

70. Roser, M., Ritchie, H. & Ortiz-Ospina, E. Internet. *Our World in Data* (2015).

71. Lorig, K. R., Ritter, P. L., Laurent, D. D. & Plant, K. The internet-based arthritis self-management program: A one-year randomized trial for patients with arthritis or fibromyalgia. *Arthritis Care Res (Hoboken)* **59**, 1009–1017 (2008).

72. Fox, S. *The Engaged E-patient Population*. (Pew Research Center, 2008). www.pewresearch.org/internet/2008/08/26/the-engaged-e-patient-population/.

73. Fox, S. & Duggan, M. *Information Triage*. (Pew Research Center, 2013). www.pewresearch.org/internet/2013/01/15/information-triage/.

74. Wong, C., Harrison, C., Britt, H. & Henderson, J. Patient use of the internet for health information. *Aust Fam Phys* **43**, 875–877 (2014).

75. Kirsch, S. E. & Lewis, F. M. Using the World Wide Web in health-related intervention research. A review of controlled trials. *Comput Inform Nurs* **22**, 8–18 (2004).

76. Kravitz, R. L. & Bell, R. a. Media, messages, and medication: Strategies to reconcile what patients hear, what they want, and what they need from medications. *BMC Med Inform Decis Mak* **13**, S5 (2013).

77. Chou, W. Y. S., Hunt, Y. M. & Beckjord, E. B. Social media use in the United States: Implications for health communication. *J Med Internet Res* **11**, e48 (2009).

78. Egilman, D. & Druar, N. M. Spin your science into gold: Direct to consumer marketing within social media platforms. *Work* **41**, 4494–4502 (2012).

79. Vozenilek, G. The wheat from the chaff: Sorting out nutrition information on the internet. *J Am Diet Assoc* **98**, 1270 (1998).

80. Levi, R. Assessing the quality of medical web sites. *Skeptical Inquirer* **24**(2), 41–45 (2000).

81. Eysenbach, G. & Diepgen, T. L. Towards quality management of medical information on the internet: Evaluation, labelling, and filtering of information. *Br Med J* **317**, 1496–1500. Preprint at https://doi.org/10.1136/bmj.317.7171.1496 (1998).

82. Culver, J. D., Gerr, F. & Frumkin, H. Medical information on the internet: A study of an electronic bulletin board. *J Gen Intern Med* **12**, 466–470 (1997).

83. Suarez-Lledo, V. & Alvarez-Galvez, J. Prevalence of health misinformation on social media: Systematic review. *J Med Internet Res* **23**, e17187. Preprint at https://doi.org/10.2196/17187 (2021).

84. Stacey, D., Légaré, F., Lewis, K., et al. Decision aids for people facing health treatment or screening decisions. *Cochrane Database Syst Rev.* doi:10.1002/14651858.CD001431.pub4 (2014).

85. Fox, S. The social life of health information, 2011. *Pew Internet Am Life Project* 1–33. doi: www.who.int/topics/tuberculosis/en/ (2011). Last Accessed: 3 February 2024.

86. Eysenbach, G. & Köhler, C. How do consumers search for and appraise health information on the world wide web? Qualitative study using focus groups, usability tests, and in-depth interviews. *BMJ* **324**, 573–577 (2002).

87. Anderson, E. L., Steen, E. & Stavropoulos, V. Internet use and Problematic Internet Use: A systematic review of longitudinal research trends in adolescence and emergent adulthood. *Int J Adolesc Youth* **22**, 430–454 (2017).

88. Fast, A. M., Deibert, C. M., Hruby, G. W. & Glassberg, K. I. Evaluating the quality of Internet health resources in pediatric urology. *J Pediatr Urol* **9**, 151–156 (2013).

89. Ahmad, F., Hudak, P. L., Bercovitz, K., Hollenberg, E. & Levinson, W. Are physicians ready for patients with internet-based health information? *J Med Internet Res* **8**, e22 (2006).

90. Berland, G. K., Elliott, M. N., Morales, L. S., et al. Health information on the Internet: Accessibility, quality, and readability in English and Spanish. *JAMA* **285**, 2612–2621 (2001).

91. Gauld, R. & Williams, S. Use of the internet for health information: A study of Australians and New Zealanders. *Inform Health Soc Care* **34**, 149–158 (2009).

92. Sommerhalder, K., Abraham, A., Zufferey, M. C., Barth, J. & Abel, T. Internet information and medical consultations: Experiences from patients' and physicians' perspectives. *Patient Educ Couns* **77**, 266–271 (2009).

93. Oliver, J. E. & Wood, T. Medical conspiracy theories and health behaviors in the United States. *JAMA Intern Med* **174**, 817–818. Preprint at https://doi.org/10.1001/jamainternmed.2014.190 (2014).

94. Schulz, P. J. & Nakamoto, K. Patient behavior and the benefits of artificial intelligence: The perils of 'dangerous' literacy and illusory patient empowerment. *Patient Educ Couns* **92**, 223–228 (2013).

95. Guyatt, G., Oxman, A. D., Kunz, R., et al. What is 'quality of evidence' and why is it important to clinicians? *BMJ* **336**, 995–998 (2008).

96. Hoffmann, T. C., Bakhit, M., Durand, M.-A., et al. Basing information on comprehensive, critically appraised, and up-to-date syntheses of the scientific evidence: An update from the international patient decision aid standards. *Med Decis Making* **41**, 755–767 (2021).

97. Tonelli, M. R. Integrating evidence into clinical practice: An alternative to evidence-based approaches. *J Eval Clin Pract* **12**, 248–256 (2006).

98. Williams, M. *Problems of Knowledge: A Critical Introduction to Epistemology.* (Oxford University Press, 2001).

99. Hunt, D. P. The concept of knowledge and how to measure it. *Journal of Intellectual Capital* **4**, 100–113 (2003).

100. Thagard, P. Explanatory coherence. *Behav Brain Sci* **12**, 435–467 (1989).

101. Haack, S. *Evidence and Inquiry: Towards Reconstruction in Epistemology.* (Blackwell Publishers Inc., 1993).

102. Douven, I. Abduction. *The Stanford Encyclopedia of Philosophy* (2021). Last Accessed: 3 February 2024.

103. Popper, K. R. *Conjectures and Refutations: The Growth of Scientific Knowledge.* (Routledge, 2002).

104. Knight, E. & Tsoukas, H. When fiction trumps truth: What 'post-truth' and 'alternative facts' mean for management studies. *Organ. Stud.* **40**, 183–197 (2019).

105. Caputo, J. D. *Truth: Philosophy in Transit.* (Penguin Books, 2013).

106. Shahrajabian, M. H., Sun, W. & Cheng, Q. Clinical aspects and health benefits of ginger (*Zingiber officinale*) in both traditional Chinese medicine and modern industry. *Acta Agric Scand, Sect B – Soil Plant Sci* **69**, 546–556. https://doi.org/10.1080/09064710.2019.1606930 (2019).

107. Ryle, G. Knowing How and Knowing That. *Proc Aristotelian Soc* **46**, 1–16 (1946).

108. Searle, J. R. *The Construction of Social Reality.* (The Free Press, 1997).

109. Searle, J. R. Wittgenstein and the background. *Am Philos Q* **48**, 119–128 (2011).

110. Vraga, E. K. & Bode, L. Defining misinformation and understanding its bounded nature: Using expertise and evidence for describing misinformation. *Polit Commun* **37**, 136–144. Preprint at https://doi.org/10.1080/10584609.2020.1716500 (2020).

111. FDA. *Vaccine Safety Questions and Answers.* FDA. (2024). www.fda.gov/vaccines-blood-biologics/safety-availability-biologics/vaccine-safety-questions-and-answers.

112. McNeil, M. M. Vaccine-associated anaphylaxis. *Curr Treat Options Allergy* **6**, 297–308. Preprint at https://doi.org/10.1007/s40521-019-00215-0 (2019).

113. US Department of Commerce, N. N. W. S. *How Dangerous Is Lightning?* (2022).

114. Lewandowsky, S., Ecker, U. K. H., Seifert, C. M., Schwarz, N. & Cook, J. Misinformation and its correction. *Psychol Sci Public Interest* **13**, 106–131 (2012).

115. Strong, S. I. Alternative facts and the post-truth society: Meeting the challenge. *Univ Pennsylvania Law Rev Online* **165**, (2017).

116. Constitution of the World Health Organization. Last Accessed: 3 February 2024. www.who.int/about/governance/constitution.

117. Shepherd, S. & Kay, A. C. On the perpetuation of ignorance: System dependence, system justification, and the motivated avoidance of sociopolitical information. *J Pers Soc Psychol* **102**, 264–280 (2012).

118. Davis, T. C., Crouch, M. A., Long, S. W., et al. Rapid assessment of literacy levels of adult primary care patients. *Fam Med* **23**, 433–5 (1991).

119. Baker, D. W., Williams, M. V., Parker, R. M., Gazmararian, J. A. & Nurss, J. Development of a brief test to measure functional health literacy. *Patient Educ Couns* **38**, 33–42 (1999).

120. Weiss, B. D., Mays, M. Z., Martz, W., et al. Quick assessment of literacy in primary care: The newest vital sign. *Ann Fam Med* **3**, 514–522 (2005).

121. Baccolini, V., Rosso, A., Di Paolo, C., et al. What is the prevalence of low health literacy in European Union Member States? A systematic review and meta-analysis. *J Gen Intern Med* **36**, 753–761. Preprint at https://doi.org/10.1007/s11606-020-06407-8 (2021).

122. National Institutes of Health. *Clear communication: Health Literacy.* www.nih.gov/clearcommunication/healthliteracy.htm (2021).

123. Sørensen, K., van den Broucke, S., Fullam, J., et al. Health literacy and public health: A systematic review and integration of definitions and models. *BMC Public Health* **12**, 80 (2012).

124. Ishikawa, H. & Kiuchi, T. Health literacy and health communication. *Biopsychosoc Med* **4**, 18. doi:10.1186/1751-0759-4-18 (2010).

125. Schwartz, L. M., Woloshin, S. & Welch, H. G. Can patients interpret health information? An assessment of the medical data interpretation test. *Med Decis Mak* **25**, 290–300. Preprint at https://doi.org/10.1177/0272989X05276860 (2005).

126. Vraga, E. K. & Tully, M. News literacy, social media behaviors, and skepticism toward information on social media. *Inf Commun Soc* **24**, 150–166 (2021).

127. Glaser, J., Nouri, S., Schenker, Y., et al. Interventions to improve patient comprehension in informed consent for medical and surgical procedures: An updated systematic review. *Med Decis Mak* **40**, 119–143. Preprint at https://doi.org/10.1177/0272989X19896348 (2020).

128. Cowburn, G. & Stockley, L. Consumer understanding and use of nutrition labelling: A systematic review. *Public Health Nutr* **8**, 21–28 (2005).

129. Bookari, K., Yeatman, H. & Williamson, M. Falling short of dietary guidelines – What do Australian pregnant women really know? A cross sectional study. *Women Birth* **30**, 9–17 (2017).

130. Sørensen, K., van den Broucke, S., Pelikan, J. M., et al. Measuring health literacy in populations: Illuminating the design and development process of the European Health Literacy Survey Questionnaire (HLS-EU-Q). *BMC Public Health* **13**, 948 (2013).

131. Carlson, J. P., Vincent, L. H., Hardesty, D. M. & Bearden, W. O. Objective and subjective knowledge relationships: A quantitative analysis of consumer research findings. *J Consum Res* **35**, 864–876 (2009).

132. Tyreman, S. The expert patient: Outline of UK government paper. *Med Health Care Philos* **8**, 149–151 (2005).

133. Ahluwalia, S., Murray, E., Stevenson, F., Kerr, C. & Burns, J. 'A heartbeat moment': Qualitative study of GP views of patients bringing health

information from the internet to a consultation. *Br J Gen Pract* **60**, 88–94 (2010).

134. van de Belt, T. H., Engelen, L. J., Berben, S. A., et al. Internet and social media for health-related information and communication in health care: Preferences of the Dutch general population. *J Med Internet Res* **15**, (2013).

135. Wason, P. C. Reasoning about a rule. *Q J Exp Psychol* **20**, 273–281 (1968).

136. Nickerson, R. S. Confirmation bias: A ubiquitous phenomenon in many guises. *Rev Gen Psychol* **2**, 175–220 (1998).

137. Suzuki, M. & Yamamoto, Y. Analysis of relationship between confirmation bias and web search behavior. In *ACM International Conference Proceeding Series* 184–191 (Association for Computing Machinery, 2020). doi:10.1145/3428757.3429086.

138. White, R. W. Beliefs and biases in web search. In *SIGIR 2013 – Proceedings of the 36th International ACM SIGIR Conference on Research and Development in Information Retrieval* 3–12 (ACM, 2013). doi:10.1145/2484028.2484053.

139. Slater, M. D. Reinforcing spirals: The mutual influence of media selectivity and media effects and their impact on individual behavior and social identity. *Commun Theory* **17**, 281–303 (2007).

140. Cinelli, M., de Francisci Morales, G., Galeazzi, A., Quattrociocchi, W. & Starnini, M. The echo chamber effect on social media. *Proc Natl Acad Sci USA* **118**, e2023301118 (2021).

141. Suzuki, M. & Yamamoto, Y. Characterizing the influence of confirmation bias on web search behavior. *Front Psychol* **12**, 5390 (2021).

142. Meppelink, C. S., Smit, E. G., Fransen, M. L. & Diviani, N. 'I was right about vaccination': Confirmation bias and health literacy in online health information seeking. *J Health Commun* **24**, 129–140 (2019).

143. Epstein, W., Glenberg, A. M. & Bradley, M. M. Coactivation and comprehension: Contribution of text variables to the illusion of knowing. *Mem Cognit* **12**, 355–360 (1984).

144. Alter, A. L., Oppenheimer, D. M. & Zemla, J. C. Missing the trees for the forest: A construal level account of the illusion of explanatory depth. *J Pers Soc Psychol* **99**, 436–451 (2010).

145. Watts, W. E., Rush, K. & Wright, M. Evaluating first-year nursing students' ability to self-assess psychomotor skills using videotape. *Nurs Educ Perspect* **30**, 214–219 (2009).

146. Kruger, J. & Dunning, D. Unskilled and unaware of it: How difficulties in recognizing one's own incompetence lead to inflated self-assessments. *J Pers Soc Psychol* **77**, 1121–1134 (1999).

147. Motta, M., Callaghan, T. & Sylvester, S. Knowing less but presuming more: Dunning–Kruger effects and the endorsement of anti-vaccine policy attitudes. *Soc Sci Med* **211**, 274–281 (2018).

148. Rappaport, J. Terms of empowerment/exemplars of prevention: Toward a theory for community psychology. *Am J Community Psychol* **15**, 121–148 (1987).

149. Wallerstein, N. Empowerment to reduce health disparities. *Scand J Public Health Suppl* **59**, 72–77 (2002).

150. Flynn, D. J., Nyhan, B. & Reifler, J. The nature and origins of misperceptions: Understanding false and unsupported beliefs about politics. *Polit Psychol* **38**, 127–150 (2017).

151. Rose, K. M., Howell, E. L., Scheufele, D. A., et al. Distinguishing scientific knowledge: The impact of different measures of knowledge on genetically modified food attitudes. *Public Understand Sci* **28**, 449–467 (2019).

152. Aitken-Swan, J. & Easson, E. C. Reactions of cancer patients on being told their diagnosis. *Br Med J* **1**, 779–783 (1959).

153. Gaston, C. M. & Mitchell, G. Information giving and decision-making in patients with advanced cancer: A systematic review. *Soc Sci Med* **61**, 2252–2264 (2005).

154. Baile, W. F., Buckman, A., Lenzi, R., et al. SPIKES – A six-step protocol for delivering bad news: Application to the patient with cancer. *Oncologist* **5**, 302–311 (2000).

155. Brashier, N. M. & Marsh, E. J. Judging truth. *Annu Rev Psychol* **71**, 499–515 (2020).

156. Schwarz, N. & Jalbert, M. When (fake) news feels true: Intuitions of truth and the acceptance and correction of misinformation. In *The Psychology of Fake News: Accepting, Sharing, and Correcting Misinformation* 73–89 (Taylor and Francis, 2020). doi:10.4324/9780429295379-7.

157. Wellin, E. Water boiling in a Peruvian town. In *Health, Culture, and Community* (ed. Paul, B. D.) 71–103 (Russell Sage Foundation, 1955).

158. Tversky, A. & Kahneman, D. Judgment under uncertainty: Heuristics and biases. *Science (1979)* **185**, 1124–1131 (1974).

159. Hasher, L., Goldstein, D., Toppino, T. Frequency and the conference of referential validity. *J Verb Learn Verb Behav* **16**, 107–112. www.sciencedirect.com/science/article/pii/S0022537177800121 (1977).

160. Fazio, L. K., Brashier, N. M., Keith Payne, B. & Marsh, E. J. Knowledge does not protect against illusory truth. *J Exp Psychol Gen* **144**, 993–1002 (2015).

161. Pornpitakpan, C. The persuasiveness of source credibility: A critical review of five decades' evidence. *J Appl Soc Psychol* **34**, 243–281 (2004).
162. Ecker, U. K. H., Lewandowsky, S., Cook, J., et al. The psychological drivers of misinformation belief and its resistance to correction. *Nat Rev Psychol* **1**, 13–29 (2022).
163. Lerner, J. S., Li, Y., Valdesolo, P. & Kassam, K. S. Emotion and decision making. *Annu Rev Psychol* **66**, 799–823 (2015).
164. Ferrer, R., Klein, W., Lerner, J., Reyna, V. & Keltner, D. Emotions and health decision making. In *Behavioral Economics and Public Health* 101–132. (Oxford University Press, 2016).
165. Higgins, E. Promotion and prevention: Regulatory focus as a motivational principle. *Adv Exp Soc Psychol* **30**, 1–46 (1998).
166. Lewandowsky, S., Ecker, U. K. H., Seifert, C. M., Schwarz, N. & Cook, J. Misinformation and its correction: Continued influence and successful debiasing. *Psychol Sci Public Interest, Suppl* **13**, 106–131 (2012).
167. Vosoughi, S., Roy, D. & Aral, S. The spread of true and false news online. *Science (1979)* **359**, 1146–1151 (2018).
168. Kricorian, K., Civen, R. & Equils, O. COVID-19 vaccine hesitancy: Misinformation and perceptions of vaccine safety. *Hum Vaccin Immunother* **18**, (2022).
169. Jennings, W., Stoker, G., Bunting, H., et al. Lack of trust, conspiracy beliefs, and social media use predict COVID-19 vaccine hesitancy. *Vaccines (Basel)* **9**, 593 (2021).
170. van Prooijen, J.-W. & Acker, M. The influence of control on belief in conspiracy theories: Conceptual and applied extensions. *Appl Cogn Psychol* **29**, 753–761 (2015).
171. March, E. & Springer, J. Belief in conspiracy theories: The predictive role of schizotypy, Machiavellianism, and primary psychopathy. *PLoS One* **14** (12), e0225964 (2019).
172. Slater, M. D. Reinforcing spirals: The mutual influence of media selectivity and media effects and their impact on individual behavior and social identity. *Commun Theory* **17**, 281–303 (2007).
173. Fransen, M. L., Smit, E. G. & Verlegh, P. W. J. Strategies and motives for resistance to persuasion: An integrative framework. *Front Psychol* **6**, 1201 (2015).
174. Bernhardt, K. L., Kinnear, T. C. & Mazis, M. B. A field study of corrective advertising effectiveness. *J Public Policy Mark* **5**, 146–162 (1986).
175. Capella, M. L., Taylor, C. R. & Webster, C. The effect of cigarette advertising bans on consumption: A meta-analysis. *J Advert* **37**, 7–18 (2008).

176. Chan, M.P.S., Jones, C. R., Hall Jamieson, K. & Albarracín, D. Debunking: A meta-analysis of the psychological efficacy of messages countering misinformation. *Psychol Sci* **28**, 1531–1546 (2017).

177. McGuire, W. J. Resistance to persuasion conferred by active and passive prior refutation of the same and alternative counterarguments. *J Abnorm Soc Psychol* **63**, 326–332 (1961).

178. Ackoff, R. L. & Emshoff, J. R. Advertising research at Anheuser-Busch, Inc. (1963–1968). *Sloan Manage Rev* **16**, 1–15 (1975).

179. Weilbacher, W. M. How advertising effects consumers. *J Advert Res* **43**, 230–234 (2003).

180. Potter, W. J. The state of media literacy. *J Broadcast Electron Media* **54**, 675–696 (2010).

181. Masur, P. K., DiFranzo, D. & Bazarova, N. N. Behavioral contagion on social media: Effects of social norms, design interventions, and critical media literacy on self-disclosure. *PLoS One* **16**, (2021).

182. Boyer, C. The internet and health: International approaches to evaluating the quality of web-based health information. In *eHealth: Legal, Ethical and Governance Challenges* (eds. Carlisle, G., Whitehouse, D. & Duquenoy, P.) 245–274 (Springer-Verlag, 2013). doi:10.1007/978-3-642-22474-4_11.

183. Purcell, G., Wilson, P. & Delamothe, T. The quality of health information on the internet: As for any other medium it varies widely; regulation is not the answer. *BMJ* **324**, 557 (2002).

184. Armstrong, K. ChatGPT : US lawyer admits using AI for case research. *BBC News* (2023).

185. Tan, S. S. L. & Goonawardene, N. Internet health information seeking and the patient-physician relationship: A systematic review. *J Med Internet Res* **19**. Preprint at https://doi.org/10.2196/jmir.5729 (2017).

186. Entralgo, P. L. *Mind and Body, Psychosomatic Pathology a Short History of the Evolution of Medical Thought.* (Kenedy, 1955).

187. Entralgo, P. *Doctor and Patient.* (McGraw-Hill, 1969).

188. Wright, E., Holcombe, C. Doctors' communication of trust, care, and respect in breast cancer: Qualitative study. *BMJ* **328**, 864 (2004).

189. Wieland, W. *Strukturwandel der Medizin und ärztlichen Ethik.* (Carl Winter Universitatsverlag, 1988).

190. Shorter, E. *Bedside manners: The troubled history of doctors and patients.* (Viking, 1985).

191. Blendon, R. J., Benson, J. M. & Hero, J. O. Public Trust in Physicians – U.S. Medicine in International Perspective. *N Engl J Med* **371**, 1570–1572 (2014).

192. Baker, R., Mainous, A. G., Gray, D. P. & Love, M. M. Exploration of the relationship between continuity, trust in regular doctors and patient satisfaction with consultations with family doctors. *Scand J Prim Health Care* **21**, 27–32 (2003).

193. Rowe, R. & Calnan, M. Trust relations in health care – The new agenda. *Eur J Public Health* **16**, 4–6 (2006).

194. Guo, H., Hildon, Z., Loh, V. W. K., et al. Exploring antibiotic prescribing in public and private primary care settings in Singapore: A qualitative analysis informing theory and evidence-based planning for value-driven intervention design. *BMC Fam Pract* **22**, 1–14 (2021).

195. Roter, D. & Hall, J. *Doctors Talking with Patients/Patients Talking with Doctors: Improving Communication in Medical Visits*. (Greenwood Publishing Group, 2006).

196. Caiata-Zufferey, M., Abraham, A., Sommerhalder, K. & Schulz, P. J. Online health information seeking in the context of the medical consultation in Switzerland. *Qual Health Res* **20**, 1050–1061 (2010).

197. Jacobs, W., Amuta, A. Health information seeking in the digital age: An analysis of health information seeking behavior among US adults. *Cogent Soc Sci* **3**, 1302785 (2017).

198. Grajales, F. J., Sheps, S., Ho, K., Novak-Lauscher, H. & Eysenbach, G. Social media: A review and tutorial of applications in medicine and health care. *J Med Internet Res* **16**(2), e13 (2014).

199. Arora, V. M., Madison, S. & Simpson, L. Addressing medical misinformation in the patient-clinician relationship. *JAMA* **324**, 2367–2368 (2020).

200. Carpenter, G. S., Glazer, R. & Nakamoto, K. Meaningful brands from meaningless differentiation: The dependence on irrelevant attributes. *J Mark Res* **31**, 339–350 (1994).

201. Bernstam, E. v. , Shelton, D. M., Walji, M. & Meric-Bernstam, F. Instruments to assess the quality of health information on the World Wide Web: What can our patients actually use? *Int J Med Inform* **74**, 13–19 (2005).

202. Gagliardi, A. & Jadad, A. R. Examination of instruments used to rate quality of health information on the internet: Chronicle of a voyage with an unclear destination. *BMJ* **324**, 569–73 (2002).

203. Ge, M., Ge, M. & Helfert, M. A review of information quality research – Develop a research agenda. In *Paper Presented at the International Conference on Information Quality 2007* 76–91 (2007).

204. Ludolph, R., Allam, A. & Schulz, P. J. Manipulating Google's knowledge graph box to counter biased information processing during an online

search on vaccination: Application of a technological debiasing strategy. *J Med Internet Res* **18**, e137 (2016).

205. Impicciatore, P., Pandolfini, C., Casella, N. & Bonati, M. Reliability of health information for the public on the World Wide Web: Systematic survey of advice on managing fever in children at home [see comments]. *Br Med J* **314**, 1875–1879 (1997).

206. Kunst, H. Accuracy of information on apparently credible websites: Survey of five common health topics. *BMJ* **324**, 581–582 (2002).

207. Latthe, M., Latthe, P. M. & Charlton, R. Quality of information on emergency contraception on the Internet. *Br J Fam Plann* **26**, 39–43. Preprint at www.ncbi.nlm.nih.gov/pubmed/10781966 (2000).

208. Doupi, P. & van der Lei, J. Rx medication information for the public and the WWW: Quality issues. *Med Inform Internet Med* **24**, 171–179 (1999).

209. Li, N., Orrange, S., Kravitz, R. L. & Bell, R. A. Reasons for and predictors of patients' online health information seeking following a medical appointment. *Fam Pract* **31**, 550–556 (2014).

210. Townsend, A., Leese, J., Adam, P., et al. eHealth, participatory medicine, and ethical care: A focus group study of patients' and health care providers' use of health-related internet information. *J Med Internet Res* **17**, e155 (2015).

211. Hart, A., Henwood, F. & Wyatt, S. The role of the Internet in patient-practitioner relationships: Findings from a qualitative research study. *J Med Internet Res* **6**, e36 (2004).

212. Anderson, R. M. Patient empowerment and the traditional medical model. A case of irreconcilable differences? *Diabetes Care* **18**, 412–415 (1995).

213. Wang, X., Shi, J. & Kong, H. Online health information seeking: A review and meta-analysis. *Health Commun* **36**, 1163–1175 https://doi.org/10.1080/10410236.2020.1748829 (2020).

214. Thapa, D. K., Visentin, D. C., Kornhaber, R., West, S. & Cleary, M. The influence of online health information on health decisions: A systematic review. *Patient Educ Couns* **104**, 770–784 (2021).

215. Funnell, M. M. & Anderson, R. M. Patient empowerment: A look back, a look ahead. *Diabetes Educ* **29**, 454–458, 460, 462 passim (2003).

216. Caiata-Zufferey, M. & Schulz, P. J. Physicians' communicative strategies in interacting with internet-informed patients: Results from a qualitative study. *Health Commun* **27**, 738–749 (2012).

217. Southwell, B. G., Wood, J. L. & Navar, A. M. Roles for health care professionals in addressing patient-held misinformation beyond fact correction. *Am J Public Health* **110**, S288–S289 (2020).

218. Petrocchi, S., Iannello, P., Lecciso, F., et al. Interpersonal trust in doctor-patient relation: Evidence from dyadic analysis and association with quality of dyadic communication. *Soc Sci Med* **235**, 112391 (2019).

219. Gravel, K., Légaré, F. & Graham, I. D. Barriers and facilitators to implementing shared decision-making in clinical practice: A systematic review of health professionals' perceptions. *Implement Sci* 9:1:16. doi: 10.1186/1748-5908-1-16. (2006).

220. Charles, C. A., Whelan, T., Gafni, A., Willan, A. & Farrell, S. Shared treatment decision making: What does it mean to physicians? *J Clin Oncol* **21**, 932–936 (2003).

221. WHO Coronavirus (COVID-19) Dashboard. *WHO Coronavirus (COVID-19) Dashboard with Vaccination Data*. https://covid19.who.int/table.

222. *The New York Times*. Trust in Fauci and U.S. health agencies resilient in a new study. *The New York Times*. www.nytimes.com/2021/07/21/us/fauci-cdc-covid-misinfo.html.

223. Jamrozik, K., Fowler, G., Vessey, M., Wald, N. Placebo controlled trial of nicotine chewing gum in general practice. *Br Med J (Clin Res Ed)* **289**, 794–797. doi:10.1136/bmj.289.6448.794 (1984).

224. Wilson, D., Wood, G., Johnston, N. & Sicurella, J. Randomized clinical trial of supportive follow-up for cigarette smokers in a family practice. *Can Med Assoc J* **126**, 127–129 (1982).

225. Russell, M., Merriman, R., Stapleton, J., & Taylor, W. Effect of nicotine chewing gum as an adjunct to general practitioner's advice against smoking. *Br Med J (Clin Res Ed)* **287**, 1782–1785 (1983).

226. Ockene, J. K. Smoking intervention: The expanding role of the physician. *Am J Public Health* **77**, 782–783 (1987).

227. Peretti-Watel, P., Seror, V., Verger, P., et al. Smokers' risk perception, socioeconomic status and source of information on cancer. *Addict Behav* **39**, 1304–1310 (2014).

228. Pew Research Center. *Younger Americans Better at Telling Factual News Statements from Opinions*. www.pewresearch.org/short-reads/2018/10/23/younger-americans-are-better-than-older-americans-at-telling-factual-news-statements-from-opinions/ (2018).

229. Johnson, E. J. & Tversky, A. Affect, generalization, and the perception of risk. *J Pers Soc Psychol* 45, 20–31 (1983).

230. Schwarz, N. & Clore, G. L. Mood, misattribution, and judgments of well-being: informative and directive functions of affective states. J Pers Soc Psychol 45, 513–523 (1983).

231. Schulz, P. J. & Nakamoto, K. The perils of misinformation: When health literacy goes awry. *Nat Rev Nephrol* (2022). https://doi.org/10.1038/s41581-021-00534-z.

232. U.S. Department of Health and Human Services. "https://www.cdc.gov/tobacco/sgr/50th-anniversary/index.htm" *The health consequences of smoking—50 years of progress: A report of the surgeon general.* (Atlanta: U.S. Department of Health and Human Services, Centers for Disease Control and Prevention, National Center for Chronic Disease Prevention and Health Promotion, Office on Smoking and Health, 2014).

Acknowledgements

The problem of misinformation has been an important undercurrent to our collaborative research over the past two decades on the impacts of health communication on health literacy, empowerment, and behaviour. That research has benefitted greatly from discussions with many faculty colleagues including Sara Rubinelli, May O. Lwin, Diana Slade, Robin Woodward-Krohn, Soontae An, Hans-Bernd Brosius, Gert-Jan de Bruijn, Clelia di Serio, Kate Hye Eun Lee, Antonio Malgaroli, and Jürgen Wilke. Of particular importance have been the thoughts and insights provided by Martha Wunsch MD who has many times offered a clinical researcher's counterpoint to our academic perspectives. Dr Uwe Hartung and Ms Teresa Cafaro helped us over many years to organize our work, granting us the most precious resource for research collaboration – time, and Albino Zgraggen of the USI administration has been unfailingly supportive of our work. The Swiss National Science Foundation, the Swiss Federal Office for Public Health, and the Humanities Research Centre at Australian National University provided funding critical to our research. In developing the present work, the reviewers for Cambridge University Press provided most valuable suggestions for improvement.

Cambridge Elements ☰

Health Communication

Louise Cummings

The Hong Kong Polytechnic University

Louise Cummings is Professor in the Department of English and Communication at The Hong Kong Polytechnic University. She conducts research in health communication and clinical linguistics and is the author and editor of over 20 books in these areas. Prof. Cummings is a member of the Royal College of Speech and Language Therapists and the Health & Care Professions Council in the UK.

About the Series

This series brings together a wide range of disciplines that converge on the study of communication in health settings. Each element examines a key topic in health communication and is carefully crafted by experts in their respective disciplines. The series is relevant to students, researchers, and practitioners in humanities, medical and health professions, and social scientific disciplines.

Cambridge Elements ≡

Health Communication

Elements in the Series

Worse Than Ignorance: The Challenge of Health Misinformation
Peter J. Schulz and Kent Nakamoto

Printed in the United States
by Baker & Taylor Publisher Services